Praise for Dogs, God and UFOs

As Mady Tobias journeys along the path to spirituality she is entrenched in an oppressive cult for ten years. In a battle for her own survival she makes the journey from victim to survivor to psychotherapist helping others. Along the way, she learns that personal trauma is a great teacher for successfully treating the military veteran victims of war. What next? The New Age and UFOs! Witty and riveting!

Kathleen Marden Author of "Fact, Fiction, and Flying Saucers" and "Captured! The Betty and Barney Hill UFO Experience"

I've known Mady Tobias since 1990. She has always been a lively, insightful, and fun colleague to be around! She embraces life with love and enthusiasm. Her personality comes through in this book, which is simultaneously interesting, delightful, and stimulating. Get to know Mady. Enjoy!

Michael Langone, Ph.D., Executive Director of the International Cultic Studies Association.

With love to Ed, whose strength and integrity made this all possible.

We are the flowers of the world
Strong but delicate
Beautiful, nurturing
Bountiful and generous
Sensitive and so easily hurt, but indestructible.

Table of Contents

Preface xiii
Prologue: A Classical Alien Abduction xvii

Part 1: The Early Years (or My Spiritual Babyhood) 1
April 1952 3
In the Beginning 9
My Grandparents 15
The Landaus. 19
Dad 23
Mom 25
Born in the Bronx 27
The Visitation. 33
I Get My Dog!. 35
Nursing School. 37
First Death 39
My Intro to the Mind 41
Choices to Make. 45
The Beach 49
Fetus or Infant? 51
Would You Marry Me? 55
Connecticut 59
Motherhood. 61

Part 2: Jewish to Christian to Cult 65
Weed! 67
Transcendental Meditation 71

My First Cult. 73
First Hypnotic Regression 77
The American Red Cross. 79
Father Ted: Intro to Catholicism 81
Into the New Age. 85
Deaths and Ghosts. 87
Chase 89
Partnership with My Guru. 93
Dr. Mady and Dr. Chase. 97
The Shelf Is Cracking 101
One Cult Was Just Not Enough. 107

Part 3: Freedom and Recovery. 111
Family First. 113
Our Clients Are Victims Too. 117
The Long Road to Recovery 119
Cult? What's That?. 123
A Healing Regression for Understanding 125
The Cult Awareness Network 129
Was Chase a Psychopath? 131
Exit Counseling vs. Deprogramming .135
Don't Call Me Doctor 139
The Dark Side 141
No End of Learning. 143
Forgiveness. 145

Part 4: Way Up North to Vermont 147
New Hampshire and Catholic Again?. 149
Vermont, the Green Mountain State .155
The Vet Center. 159
EMDR and Post-Traumatic Stress Disorder 165
9/11 and the Team 171
Manhattan 175
Women Are Veterans Too! 179
Fire!. 181

Angels to the Rescue! 185
Insomnia and PTSD. 193
Dogs and Horses for Heroes. 195
PTSD? Me? 199

Part 5: Retirement and Back to the New Age. 201
Horses, Angels, and Helicopters. 203
Next "Job": Loudon County Medical Reserve Corps. 207
Second Hypnotic Regression 211
Hospice and Reiki 213
Animal Communication 221
Poltergeist. 227
Dogfight 229
Virginia Master Naturalists 231

Part 6: Dulce and UFOs 235
Dulce and the UFO Highway 237
MUFON: The Mutual UFO Network 243
Dulce UFO Conference. 245
Another Regression 247
MUFON and the Experiencer Research Team 249
Another Regression? 253
Into the Stars 257
Jacquelin Smith 259
Debra's Story 265
Kids and UFOs. 269
A Few Words of Advice 273
What's Next?. 275

Conclusion 279
Acknowledgments 281
Appendix 283
Bibliograpy. 287
Suggested Reading. 291

Preface

"Go let them out," said Mary, our next-door neighbor, as her dogs crowded to the screen door. We had just finished dinner, and I opened the door and watched the four large Norwegian Elkhounds and the three Russell terriers, all retired champion show dogs, run out into the large fenced-in yard.

I stepped outside to watch them as they ran to the far corner of the yard and started barking and growling. Then I heard one of them yelping in pain and fear as they jumped on something they caught. Too far away to see what they'd gotten, I walked over, curious at the commotion.

I stopped cold, shocked in horror as I saw them attacking one of their own—an elderly Elkhound bitch. I rapidly strode out to them, my arms outstretched, and commanded them firmly, loudly, and repeatedly, "Get back! Get back now!"

They stopped what they were doing, looked up at me, and immediately obeyed my commands to back off. I walked to the grounded dog, expecting her to be horribly wounded, but she slowly got up and came with me back to the house. The others followed at a good distance behind, as I reminded them to get back when they got too close.

Mary and Ed were stunned. And so was I.

"You shouldn't have let them all out!" she said. Now she tells me!

"Has this ever happened before?" I asked.

"Yes, just once. I had to break up the fight by beating them with a broom!" she explained. Having learned that painful lesson, she now only let them out a few at a time. Too bad she hadn't told *me* that!

I have no idea why and how my approach worked. I know that dog fights, even between just two dogs, are a dangerous thing for anyone to try and stop. I had seen videos on "safe ways" to stop two dogs from fighting when they were still attached to their owners' leashes, always with warnings to those who might try.

I had heard of owners who'd been attacked and seriously injured while trying to separate their dogs from fighting with other dogs. I'd never seen a video of a pack fight.

In any case, I was not thinking anything at the time. I was in an altered state. As I stared intently at the dogs, I felt powerful and full of an authority I'd never known. What *really* happened?

I have always felt different from everyone else. Doesn't everyone feel that way? Since 1979, when I began my career as a psychotherapist, I have wondered, and have been *in* wonder, at how we are all the same and yet all different from each other.

I have met both good and perhaps evil human beings, some of whom you will meet in this book. I don't like the word evil, and yet it signifies to me a profound badness. The few that I have personally encountered fall into that category. They may just as easily be described as having an antisocial personality disorder, as defined by the American Psychiatric Association, or as sociopathic. However, that does not describe the immense psychological toll their greed and anger inflected upon me, my family, and others.

But this book is not about them. No, on the contrary, it's about the opposite, about the profound goodness I have discovered in this life. Perhaps it has been necessary to encounter the bad in order to appreciate the good. This book is about growth, my growth, from innocence to awareness. Awareness that continues to grow with age and awe. An awareness beyond the boundaries of mind and body.

I began writing this book in order to comprehend the connections I was having with animals, humans, and even extraterrestrials. How did this happen? When did this begin? Only when I began to write down my story for myself did I start to understand what that little girl from the Bronx had to do with this retiree in Virginia.

What I didn't know was that all my weird experiences in life were connected. And I didn't see the connections until I wrote them down.

How did I get absorbed into the world of ufology, belief in extraterrestrial life, and contact with nonhuman intelligences? What does this have to do with my spirituality and spiritual growth?

What about the paranormal events, psychic phenomena, and reincarnation memories? This book began as an attempt to bring these seemingly disparate parts of myself and my experiences into meaningful coexistence. I had no idea of the size and depth of the community of like-minded individuals I would discover who were also searching for answers. This book is for them.

In the prologue, I begin with one of the most interesting and compelling cases that I encountered in my volunteer work with the Mutual UFO Network's Experiencer Research Team (MUFON ERT). These two women tell about their mutual encounter with nonhuman intelligent beings aboard a spacecraft and their difficulties coming to terms with their experience. They urged me to tell their story, with their identities protected.

In the following chapters, I share stories of my own growth, psychological, spiritual, and cosmic, which led me to this work. Dogs, God, and UFOs have followed me throughout my life, even when I didn't know the meanings of my experiences. I share this in support of those countless others who have told me their own stories, fears, and revelations.

My love for all animals has influenced me throughout my life. I include dogs in the title, but I could just as easily have said cats, horses, black panthers, birds, or any of the myriad animals I have been blessed to encounter. They were all important in my growth.

I originally wrote this book for my grandson and then realized that I wrote it for myself. To understand who I was. It worked. I could now shelve it, work done. Why go to the bother of countless edits and figuring out how to publish it?

Then I thought, if it helps but one other person discover who they are and why they are here on this wonderful world, this effort will be worthwhile.

I have found that, as Mark Twain supposedly said, "The two most important days of your life are the day you were born and the day you find out why."

To my surprise, I am still finding that out.

Prologue

A Classical Alien Abduction

The following abduction report was made to the Mutual UFO Network in 2014. This is from the MUFON field investigator's original report of the incident, found in the MUFON Case Management System (CMS). My comments follow and are a result of contact with these two ladies four years later. All identifying data has been removed to protect the witnesses' identity and privacy. I have not corrected for typos and misspellings, but in my comments describing my interviews, I have made minor changes to the witnesses' email messages for readability.

Synopsis from the CMS report:

"My friend and I were sitting on her deck drinking coffee. She said, "Look!" I looked up in time to see a rectangular shaped object with lights circling around it, changing colors. We kept saying, "What is that?" It briefly went totally dark and then reappeared moving toward her property. Her house is situated at an elevation of 1,053 feet above sea level according to my phone. There is a VERY STEEP drop off at the edge of her lawn which is heavily wooded all the way down the mountain. These objects were high above the trees which are very tall. As the large object moved closer and closer to us a small semi-circular shaped object was see below the larger object. I grabbed my cell phone and began taking photos of what we were seeing. It came close enough to her lawn to reflect light onto the grass. Then the semi-circular shaped object straightened itself out, as is seen in the photo, and flew at a speed I've never seen anything move with out of our sight behind trees. It did not return that we saw. The large object began getting very bright with almost fiery looking lights shooting out of the ring where the multi-colored lights were first observed. We watched it for what seemed like a short period of time but we later realized we had been out there watching for about an hour and a half. I have no direct memory of the object leaving or blinking out but it was just gone. I began to take photos all around in hopes of finding where it went. That's when I got the very poor photo of what seems to be two little creatures. Also, strangely enough another glowing light appeared deep down in the woods. It would brighten when we talked to it and dim and then brighten again on request. My camera never recorded a photo of this object although I snapped them repeatedly. My friend said once during watching the object she was going to get a flashlight and go out there and look more closely. I strongly encouraged her not to do that. I felt that we were fine on the deck where we were but didn't need to be out there any closer. We were unnaturally calm afterward and even talked about how we just sauntered back inside the house and went to bed - too calm if you ask me. Odd."

Object Description:
Size of Object:
Basketball size.
Distance from Object:
87 feet. 145 Magnetic Degree.
Direction Object was first Observed:
North.
Direction Object was last Observed:
North.
Observed Flight/Movement Characteristics of Object:

According to both witnesses, the object had a hovering path and no landing was observed. No emission or sound. Had a white surface and gold/ copper, pink/rose, yellow/orange, yellow, and blue/green exterior lights.

<u>Witness Illustrations/Pictures:</u>
Exhibit 1:

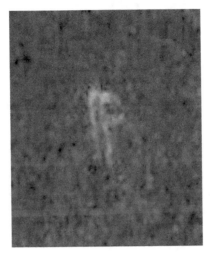

Aliens Picture – according to witnesses.

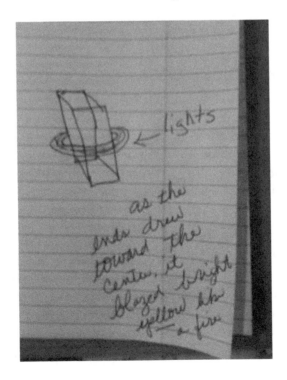

INVESTIGATOR NARRATIVE:

Witness Interviews/Statements Regarding Unknown Object: I contacted both witnesses by email, phone, and in person. I visited the actual location of the event in November 1, 2014. I spoke with both witnesses at the site. According to them, they were in the front deck of one of the witness' home drinking decaf coffee and sweet tea with lemon after celebrating one of the witness's birthday. Both told me that have not drink any alcohol that day. The only medications that one of the witnesses is taking are for arthritis and blood pressure. Both wear glasses and don't have any vision impairment. They acted normal around me. Both started to tell me about their event. According to them, around 10:45 pm, one of the witnesses noticed a small light coming to them and told to the other witness. Both saw like a small light hovering in front of the deck, about 87 feet, and immediately one of them started to take pictures, no videos, of the object. Suddenly, the light changed shape to a big rectangular shape and lights were turning around the object. After that, both witnesses lost time. They don't remember what happened until one of them did a hypnosis with a friend of one of the witnesses' sister. According to the hypnosis and the witness, both of them were taken into a mother ship that was flying over the clouds and the ocean during daylight. Inside the spaceship the witness saw a big table that have gross things like raw meats and body animal parts. Also, she observed two aliens with big eyes. Their eyes were similar to the pupil of a cat. They were between 5'7" and 6' high. They look like reptiles. Later, observed 4 more aliens, possible females, with curly and tangle hairs. Their cloths were tight to their bodies. She can hear them talking to themselves saying that she was old but their mouths were always closed. Their skin color was tan. They tried to conduct an examination on her but they stopped because she wasn't cooperating, screaming and kicking. They gave her a tranquilizer to calm her down. Later in that night both wake up back in the front deck naked and feeling wear. They notice the time was around 1:30 am. For last, one of the witnesses was recording the conversation and interviewed without asking or letting me know. I was curious about that.

Witness Interviews/Statements Regarding Post Sighting Anomalies: After the event one of the witnesses have 2 bruises in both upper arms (1 each round points). The same witness had vocal cords problems and had a surgery in a later day. Actually, she is feeling much better. The other witness didn't want to do the hypnosis because she wants to forget about the event. Both have nightmares and can't sleep well. One of the witness told me that the aliens went back to see her at her home during the night when she was sleeping and confront her for not keeping her mouth closed.

Investigation Findings: It is the opinion of FI...that the event that was witnessed by these two ladies was an unknown. The location and time of the event were perfect for an abduction. The photos taken were not good enough. I believed those photos can be replicate by humans. I have doubts about the event but because I don't have sufficient proof about what really happened. It is their words against my opinion. Probably really happened or maybe not. Could be a hoax.

<u>**Witness Credibility:**</u>
Unknown.
<u>**Correlating Cases:**</u>
There are no correlating cases in the CMS at this time.
<u>**Investigation Status:**</u>
Completed.
<u>**Case Disposition:**</u>
Unknown – Other.

"State Director comments: Photos are not original ones. No EXIF data found. Photos are also very poor quality. Lights show motion blurring. Witness did not provide other witness names and information. If this was this incredible, why are they being so nonchalant about this and delayed telling someone?"

A Learning Moment: Melinda and Norma's Account

The MUFON Experiencer Research Team was formed in 2015 under the direction of Kathleen Marden to do both research on the abduction phenomena and to assist those whose who reported encounters with Non-Human Intelligences (NHIs). Those who wished assistance with their experiences were encouraged to fill out the Experience Questionnaire on the MUFON website. (See Appendix).

When Melinda filled out a questionnaire in 2018, four years after her original CMS report, it was then sent on to me for follow-up. I first looked up the CMS report of 2014, and noted that the remarks by both the field investigator and state director were somewhat derogatory and dismissive. They were not taken to be valid.

Shortly after I got the referral, I wrote to Melinda, introduced myself, and told her my job was to assist her in any way I could and to provide her with information, resources, and mostly support.

She responded to my email introduction the same day, writing, "I spend a lot of my time trying to forget my experience or talking myself into believing it was a dream…except a school mate was visiting that weekend for our monthly class of 1968 breakfast. All my life my family has seen small lights on our property—we actually thought they were a ghost. Before my experience, my friend also saw this light, and my sister had seen it two days earlier. My house is on top of a mountain, wooded and excluded. Except for my beautiful view of other mountains, we have no close neighbors.

"My friend Norma and I were on my front porch with a cup of coffee around 10ish that night. My dogs started barking furiously and ran to the edge of the woods. Then they became silent and left the yard. The crickets and frogs—everything became silent. Norma saw the light coming from the sky; I don't remember seeing it until it appeared in the yard. It looked to be as large as a basketball, first with a gold ring circling it, then changing colors and shapes. Once it even looked as though it had a face. Then a smaller light appeared underneath it. It illuminated the grass. It was small and glowed, not giving out light like a flashlight but glowing. My friend had a good cell phone, and she started taking pictures.

I decided I would go investigate it. She panicked and begged me not to go, saying that she had a bad feeling about it.

"The smaller one left first, and it looked like a shooting star, just a light trail going up toward the mountains in the distance. The big light just shut down. I don't remember seeing it leave. I would never have mentioned this experience to anyone, *except* I had pictures and a friend that experienced it along with me.

"We went inside, put our cold coffee in the sink, and said that we were tired. Norma said, 'No wonder we are tired, it's after one o'clock.' I did not connect the time lost until much, much later. I thought we were out on the porch for maybe ten minutes or so. Norma went back to her home, which is several hours away from mine. We kept in touch and realized the similarities we started experiencing, loss of sleep and terrible nightmares. I wanted to tear my clothes off my body and run, run, run. I had to go to the doctor and was put on antidepressants. Norma also had the same feelings and was having nightmares of being kidnapped. One other very strange thing that happened for several months was I actually could hear something walking on my roof, which is impossible since it is very steep. I also heard muted voices but couldn't quite make out the words. These happenings occurred when I had company, so I know it wasn't in my mind.

"After going through so much craziness, I decided to be hypnotized. My first memory was going out with coffee and sitting down and immediately seeing a very tall being. I started screaming, and the therapist brought me out. The next session I remember seeing Norma lying on a table, and a tall being was touching her face with four fingers—just four. I had the most terrible feeling of guilt, because I knew it was my fault that this was happening to her. I realize now that I probably had been taken before, but I also don't know how much I believe in hypnosis.

"I have come out of this experience believing that there is something devastating coming to our planet, and they will be here to help or start over. Under hypnosis I saw two female-looking beings that were really ugly, hair in patches and wearing dated clothing maybe from '70s or before. They looked almost like twins. I thought that maybe they were going to be living on Earth. It was nothing that was said to me but something I felt.

"I would love to know someone's theory about what is going to happen and why. I honestly wish this had never happened but know it did. Now what? I just try not to think of it and try to dismiss it. But it's hard to do when I had a friend with a camera phone.

"Thanks for listening to me, and if you know what's going on, would you please let me know?"

I spoke with Melinda at length that same day, and afterward had several communications with her by phone and email. I found her accounts of the event credible and her emotional responses appropriate. She is currently retired from a position working with the mentally handicapped. She is now sixty-eight years old. (She also sent me DVDs of her hypnosis sessions, which were as she described).

I strongly suggested that her friend fill out an Experiencer questionnaire as well, as she too has had considerable anxiety since the event. Two days later I received Norma's questionnaire from our ERT research director. Norma told me, "I have never been able to come to terms with my experience that evening." As she related what happened, she began to calm down. I try to listen empathetically and be supportive when experiencers talk about what for them is understandably very traumatic.

Norma told me she is a retired elementary school teacher. She now teaches Sunday school and sings in her church choir. She told me that on the night of the incident, she and Melinda were celebrating her sixty-fourth birthday after the class reunion. When the dogs started barking, she grabbed her phone to take pictures of the lights she saw in the sky, then snapped a picture of a tall being in front of her friend. They both then saw two beings looking at her. She did not recall taking those pictures until later when she saw them on her phone. She sent them to Melinda, and they both became very anxious and started having nightmares.

Norma told me about *her* hypnotic regression in September 2014. She described lying on a metal table and being examined by tall beings with four long fingers. She fought them, and during her struggles she was given an injection in her spine. She said they had a special interest in her neck. She had large polyps, which were scheduled to be removed in the coming week. (Incidentally, when she went in for surgery, the doctors told her they were now much smaller in size!)

After this, she looked around the ship for her clothes. She encountered "two fellows" who let her wander around. She had on only a sheet-like cloth. She saw a room with many bodily organs, some small, some very large, on a table. Some looked familiar, others not. Looking out a window, she saw only darkness and realized she was not on Earth. She started to pray. She found her clothes and with them a hypodermic syringe. She grabbed it to defend herself when suddenly a little dog walked in who looked like a pet she had had years ago! It said, "You don't want to hurt them." She gave the dog the syringe, and it turned into one of the extraterrestrials.

Norma also had a "thing" cut out of the instep of her foot. She stated that she believed it was sent to Auburn University for analysis and then on to MIT. She was not able to find out what it was, and no one admits to ever seeing it. She stated she has another lump in the instep of her other foot but has no plans at this time to have it removed. She wants to keep it for herself! Talk about a change in attitude!

Both women described the nonhuman intelligent beings (NHIBs) as between six and seven feet tall; ashy gray in color, eyes slanted up, large and dark, much bigger than human eyes; nose just two tiny holes; no lips, just a slit for a mouth. They wore light-colored robes and had four very long fingers, with no opposable thumb.

They also saw other NHIBs on the ship who appeared to be human-like, with spindly hair and dressed in '60s- and '70s-style clothing. Norma heard them say to her (telepathically), "She's old. What would they want with her?" To which she replied, "I am old, but you are ugly!" Now she can laugh at that.

Melinda and Norma described the craft as having no light fixtures, but the lighting seemed to come indirectly from the light gray walls, which were all curved.

At the end of my report to MUFON, I stated that I believe these two women, now both sixty-eight years old, to be credible witnesses. My reasons are as follows:

1. They were together and awake when they were abducted from the porch of the house.
2. Independent hypnotic regressions produced similar accounts.
3. An implant was reported to be removed.
4. They reported a loss of time of about three hours.
5. They both did volunteer work in their community and churches.
6. They had nothing to gain from making a false report.

When I asked what conclusions they had now, four years later, because of their experiences, Norma wrote to me, "I feel privileged to have had this experience. Everyone should have at least one experience they cannot explain. I love remembering and pondering what happened to us. Most of all, I wonder if I will see them again. I think I want to…maybe [smile emoji]!"

Melinda wrote, "I believe that something devastating is going to happen to this planet, and they will be there to help or start over."

It is not our position on the ERT to interpret or influence the experiencer to change their perceptions of the incident(s) but to provide support, a listening ear, and resources for them to explore. Their emotions following the incident were tumultuous. When they reported it to MUFON in 2014, they were still in a state of shock and had not come to terms with the impact of what happened. Understandably, it was incomprehensible to them. Even after four years, the fear, guilt, and depression led them to keep the full account to themselves.

I am thankful that with support, they have been able to come to come to terms with these extraordinary experiences. Increasingly field investigators and state directors are now taking advantage of Experiencer Research Team members to assist in their investigation of *all* reports of contact with nonhuman intelligent beings.

Addendum: After reviewing this article, both witnesses stated that these NHIBs were *definitely not* reptilians. And when they came back they were wearing their clothes. The photos were taken by an iPhone 4, which explains their poor quality.

The "delays" in reporting the incident were due to their lack of memory of what happened until they were hypnotized, at which point they made a report. I have their signed permissions to include their story, and though they would like to remain anonymous, they would like others to know that these events do happen!

I chose to include Melinda and Norma's account here for two reasons. First of all, it demonstrates how far MUFON, as an organization, has come since 2014 when they first made their report, in recognizing the importance and validity of those who experience encounters with NHIs. State Directors and Field Investigators are now working closely with our team on those cases. In addition, reports and accounts of abductions are being included in the monthly MUFON Journal.

As I got to know them over the next several months and help them come to terms with *their* experiences, it became clear to me that I too needed to come to terms with my *own* incredible experiences. Were they real or imaginary? What meaning, if any, do they now give to my life?

Both Melinda and Norma have encouraged me to have this published. They wish that more people were aware of the extraordinary events that have occurred and continue to occur between us earthlings and other entities in the worlds beyond ours.

Now, back to the past and my beginning!

Part 1

The Early Years (or My Spiritual Babyhood)

⟨⟩

__I Dropped a Ball__
I dropped a ball in your lap
It's time to play
I just put a ball in your lap
So it's time to play
See that ball I placed in your lap?
That means it's time to play
You can have your emergency appendectomy
Any other day
But I dropped a ball in your lap
And now it's time to play
—*Francesco Marciuliano*, I Could Chew on This: And Other Poems by Dogs

April 1952

"Owwwww! Mommy! Owwwww!"

It is still dark in our bedroom, and I push at Ina to wake her up. She is already awake and pissed at me for screaming.

"What?" Ina snaps grumpily, startled out of sleep.

Ina, five years my senior, tumbles out of the double bed we share. Alarm begins to distort her face as my screaming continues.

"It hurts," I sob, unable to move without a excruciating pain in my abdomen. "Mommy, please, it hurts."

The sound of pain and terror in my voice forces our younger brother, Eddie, awake. His bed, just feet from Ina's and mine, will not be a refuge tonight.

Frightened and confused by the noise, our mother charges into the room, throwing on the lights and bringing the urgency of my situation into clear focus.

"Mady, what's wrong?" she asks as she rushes to my bedside, throwing back the covers and searching for signs of trauma.

My mother's cool hands brush my tears away as I try to describe the incredible pain I'm in.

"It's—it's—it's my tummy. I hurt!" I stammer.

Deep on the right side of my belly, the sharp pain feels like a hot knife stabbing into me. Mom helps me to get up and use the bathroom. Sobbing with each step, beads of sweat form on my brow. In the bathroom I throw up what little is left from last night's dinner and stagger back to my bed.

3

I can hear Mom's voice from the other room speaking with our family doctor. Now I know it's bad. Mom is begging at him to get here quickly. As if the pain isn't bad enough, I hate Dr. Schweig. He always smells like disinfectant and gives me shots that hurt no matter what he says.

Ina and Eddie huddle on his bed, the color drained from their faces. Their expressions and the fear in their eyes convince me I am going to die, and I sob harder.

Waves of pain wash over me as I anxiously await the arrival of the doctor, knowing with all the certainty of a seven-year-old that something awful is happening.

He's here! I hear Mom greeting him and see her pushing him into the bedroom.

His large body appears in the doorway, and his trained eye quickly takes in my flushed face and pained expression. Gently he pulls up my pajama top, exposing my midsection as his experienced fingers press deeply and firmly on the right side of my stomach.

"Owwwww!" I howl at the pressure. Tears soak my pillow, and I can't catch my breath. This is the worst pain ever!

"She needs to go to the hospital immediately," Dr. Schweig says over his shoulder to my mom. "They have to take her appendix out."

I hear my mother inhale sharply. What's an appendix? This can't be good!

Everything happens at once, like they are playing my life as a movie but at fast-forward speed. Somebody bundles me up and carries me to the doctor's car.

"Don't worry, honey. Everything is going to be fine," Mom says, trying to sound convincing but falling short to my young ears. "Cousin Charlie is meeting us at the hospital, and he will take your appendix out."

The mention of Cousin Charlie does nothing to calm my fears. I don't remember *any* Cousin Charlie!

From the doctor's car, I am placed in a chair with wheels. Not having to walk or move helps to move the pain to the background as I take in this alien planet they call the hospital. Mechanical, crackling voices appear to be coming from the ceiling, and unidentifiable names are in great demand being sent to unidentifiable places.

"Dr. Barry, please report to the ER, stat. Dr. Barry to ER," says a nasally, high-pitched voice somewhere above us. "Dr. Edsol to the ICU. Dr. Edsol to ICU."

The lights are so bright that I must blink repeatedly to focus on the strange creatures in white robes, white masks, and funny hats whizzing by us.

Why am I here? What are they going to do to me? I'm pushed in my new chair through the hospital emergency room and admitting area, where Mom stops accompanying me on my way to another scary room.

"What are you doing?" I cry out as strangers undress me and replace my nightgown with another that has no back and barely covers me. It has no back!

"Mommy! Why can't she come? Where is she?" I cry. No one answers me.

I am zoomed right into a very strange all-white room, surrounded by silent creatures in white outfits and masks, who scurry around looking busy and moving stuff.

They lift me on to a very hard and narrow bed, and I am covered with a sheet. What is happening? No one tells me what is going on.

"We are going to take your appendix out," someone says. "But don't worry, you are going to be sound asleep and wake up in no time!" What does that mean? The smells of alcohol and other stuff are strong and scary.

My arms and legs are tied down! Why? Then a mask with something like the worst smell in the whole wide world is placed on my face. The stranger above and behind me tries to calm me down.

"It's okay, I am a friend of your daddy's. Just breathe deeply and go to sleep," he says.

I don't have any choice. The ether smells horrible, and I fight and struggle unsuccessfully to get it away. No use. But before I fade away, *I see a checkerboard of squares revolve into a vortex and pull me into it and away.*

Where did I go? What part of me left my body? The first mystery. (Decades later, I was informed that I was taken away and protected, prepared for a future of healing and more.)

I am only seven years old, yet I still remember vividly waking up from anesthesia with my arms and legs bound tightly to the bed.

"Mommy, Mommy, Mommy!" I scream, frightened and in pain. A nurse rushes in and unties me when I promise not to move much.

In my room is another child with a mysterious line attached to his arm and a bottle of fluid above him. He never talks, never moves. The next day I am able to get out of bed and wander around.

"What this? What's that? Why, why, why?" I ask everyone I encounter as I poke my head into every room, doorway, and closet. Curiosity now replaces fear. I am fascinated with everything I see: the nurses in uniform, the strange equipment in rooms, all the kids who never talk but lie quietly in their beds or cry.

"What's the matter with them?" I ask, with no answers from the nurses.

From my bed at night, I can see the wonders of the George Washington Bridge, connecting NYC and New Jersey, lit up in the dark like a Christmas tree. A hospital room with a view! Hospitals, awful but fascinating, I think.

Mom visited every day, and I couldn't wait to go home. Daddy stayed behind, caring for Eddie and Ina.

After my appendectomy, I had three very strong wishes that survive to this day.

1. I wanted knowledge of all that is knowable and unknowable. I imagined taking a special pill that would enlighten me, though I didn't know that word existed. I wanted to know everything, immediately. What, why, how, who, where, when.

2. I wanted to fly. I don't mean in an airplane. Perhaps like Superman. I went somewhere under anesthesia; I wanted to go back there and explore the unknown worlds.

3. The last wish was to have a dog. Lying alone in my bed recovering from surgery, as well as from scarlet fever, chicken pox, and measles that year, I watched a lot of television. Every episode of *The Adventures of Rin Tin Tin* and *Lassie* brought a hunger for a furry friend, protector, and soulmate. *Eternal love and acceptance.*

I could not know then that what I was wishing for was bliss, wisdom, and the ability to expand through the universe.

If nothing else, I learned that there was more to me than just my body.

In the Beginning

Dear Lucy,
Where would we be without you? What was it like there?
Why did you leave Africa?
—Mady

WHERE DID MADY BEGIN? As an adult I could find out! I could also find out if I was susceptible to diabetes, certain cancers, blood diseases, Parkinson's, and Alzheimer's, to name just a few dreaded ailments that may be genetically more likely to impale you. Since my father died of cancer, my mother of heart disease, my aunt had Alzheimer's, and too many of my family were diabetic, those were part of the halo of illnesses that swam around my brain, coming closer as I aged.

This led me to a genetic service in search of my roots and relationship to Lucy as well. Where did I come from, and do I have any Neanderthal in me?

I received my history in a special report from 23andMe, the company I sent a sample of my spit to. With that tiny sample, they traced my ancestry through my maternal DNA. I always knew that women were special from the beginning of humanity!

They told me, "Your spit contains a lot of DNA, packaged tightly inside your cells, which are the building blocks that make up all life on earth."

Okay, here we go. Lucy. The following is the report provided to me by 23 and Me:

180,000 Years Ago

If every person living today could trace his or her maternal line back over thousands of generations, **all** *of our lines would meet at a single woman (Lucy) who lived in eastern Africa between 150,000 and 200,000 years ago. The story of your [my] maternal line begins with her.*

Your maternal line refers to a unique set of genetic variations in your mitochondrial DNA that have been passed down to you for thousands of years through your maternal line— from your great-grandmother to your grandmother to your mother.

65,000 Years Ago

Your branch of Lucy arose from a woman who likely lived in eastern Africa between 60,000 and 70,000 years ago. While many of her descendants remained in Africa, one small group ventured east across the Red Sea. That means we are all African. Black, red, white, and yellow. Who knew?

59,000 Years Ago

Your story continues with one of two branches that arose in southwestern Asia. The women [and men, I assume] migrated across all of Eurasia, giving rise to new branches from Portugal to Polynesia.

10

18,000 Years Ago
Lucy's descendants expanded dramatically to the north after the Ice Age and eventually reached from Arabia to the western fringes of Siberia.

Ah, climate change! Why else did they leave Africa and spread around the world? I guess for the same reasons people leave their homes today: competition for limited resources, such as food and water; warfare; and religious persecution.

Ashkenazi Jewish*: Ashkenazi Jewish people [that's me] settled in central and eastern Europe in the late Middle Ages, but their modern descendants remain genetically more like other Jewish populations than like their European neighbors, reflecting shared western Asian origins. In the twentieth century, many Ashkenazi Jewish people immigrated to Israel or to the Americas in search of greater cultural and religious acceptance.*

"Greater cultural and religious acceptance?" You've got to be kidding. Pogroms, rape, and then genocide—the Holocaust! Why not call it what is was: horror!

The bottom line is this: as Dr. Pete Smith, Professor of Soils and Global Change, University of Aberdeen said, "People don't stay and die where they are. *All* people since Lucy have migrated, and for the same reasons: food, safety, and peace. And still do."

I needed to know more. Now that my curiosity was roused, I began some research. Since the Middle Ages, my ancestors had lived in Eastern Europe. Then disaster. On March 1, 1881, Czar Alexander II was assassinated by revolutionary terrorists. His reign was a brief episode (twenty years) in the brutal history of anti-Semitism throughout his realm. His murder brought on waves of pogroms (anti-Semitic terrorism) promoted by the new czar, Alexander III, that changed the emotional climate toward Jews throughout the Russian empire. Terror ruled.

At that time, and since the Middle Ages, Jews lived in shtetls. Irving Howe, in *World of Our Fathers: The Journey of the East European Jews to America and the Life They Found and Made* (1976), describes shtetls as small towns consisting of "a jumble of wooden houses clustered higgledy-piggledy about a market-place...as crowded as a slum...The streets...are tortuous...They are bent into question marks and folded into parentheses. They run into cul-de-sacs like a theory arrested by fact; they ooze off into lanes, alleys, back yards...[At the center] is the marketplace, with its shops, booths, tables, stands, butchers' blocks. Hither come daily, except during the winter, the peasants and peasant women from many miles around, bringing their livestock and vegetables, their fish and hides, their wagonloads of grain, melons, parsley, radishes, and garlic. They buy in exchange the city produce which the Jews import: dry goods, hats, shoes. The tumult of the market-place...is one of the wonders of the world."

The Cossacks under the czars were Russia's greatest military assets. After Alexander II's assassination, the Jews were blamed, and anti-Jewish riots swept throughout Russia to Poland. The shtetls were targeted as waves of Cossacks burned, massacred, robbed, and raped the towns. Life for this already impoverished population became horrendous. As Wikipedia explains, from 1881 until the start of WWI in 1917, thousands of Jewish men, women, and children were killed and additional hundreds of women raped.

I try to imagine the lives of my grandparents in Kiev and Galicia/ Austria. But I can't. Their life was a daily nightmare. Impoverished already, parents endlessly cried and argued whether to send their children, with or without them, on the journey through Russia to America thousands of miles away. No wonder that between 1881 and the start of WWI, nearly a third of Eastern European Jews fled their homelands in Russia, Romania, and Poland. America was a magical land of promise: food, land, safety, and the ability to practice their religion.

In Europe, selling everything of value, they said their goodbyes and took their children with but meager belongings and food and deposited them onto the wagon carts and train platforms, where they traveled alone or with small family groups on the long journey across Eastern Europe. The trips took several painful weeks whether by train or cart, or even on foot. Some families paid huge sums to smugglers to bring them and their children from the east to various ports in the west.

Refugees, they crossed the border—legally, with passports, or illegally, without them—to Germany. From there, Jewish communities raised the funds to provide transport onto the steamships that would take them to America. I don't think they wanted them to stay there either. On board, they lived below deck in steerage, crowded in, hundreds at a time, in cramped quarters, sleeping on wooden tiers, eating barely edible food, drinking foul water, and vomiting on each other for the next seven to fourteen days while crossing the Atlantic. No bathing facilities, with horrid toilets. The stench was unbearable.

Between 1895 and 1899, almost eighty thousand Jews arrived in New York Harbor and went through immigration at Ellis Island, my grandparents among them. In only eleven more years, by 1910, the number of Jews in NYC increased to about 1,100,000. I wonder if those who left without their parents, including my grandparents, ever heard from their families again.

But they were the lucky ones. In the next thirty years, culminating with the rise of Hitler, the rest of the Jewish population that failed to escape was nearly exterminated. Those fleeing via steamship and heading to the United States were turned back to Germany and the concentration camps to die. The chance to emigrate as refugees from war, starvation, and persecution was no longer a given. Not unlike today's refugees, they were labeled undesirable, Communists, or thieves and turned away.

My Grandparents

1880–1900

⟋⟍

EVER SINCE I WAS VERY young, I wondered why anyone would leave home, family, and safety. In school I learned about brave explorers like Columbus and others who "sailed the ocean blue" seeking gold and riches, who had an irresistible urge to find new lands and conquer other peoples for their kings and queens in Europe. Curiosity, greed, power, fame? Were those the only enticements to go forth into the unknown, facing the dangers of death, disease, and warfare with native peoples? Not enough enticement for me. Well, curiosity maybe.

In the sixth grade, at PS 96 in the Bronx, New York City, we learned about immigrants. Over 50 percent of my class were second-generation Jewish Americans. The rest were mostly Italian or Irish, many second- or third-generation Americans. Our parents and grandparents, we were taught in school, had come to America "for a better life." The "old" life was not defined, just the promises of a new one. We learned to sing:

> Give me your tired, your poor
> Your huddled masses yearning to breathe free
> The wretched refuse of your teeming shore
> Send these, the homeless, tempest-tossed to me,
> I lift my lamp beside the golden door.

I sang those words from Emma Lazarus's poem throughout my years in elementary school in the early '50s. I was moved by the lyrics without fully understanding them. We went on school trips to the Statue of Liberty, where those words were inscribed, and saw from a distance Ellis Island, where twelve million immigrants who came to the United States by ship went through inspection from 1892 to 1954, when the center closed.

⌣⟶

I had two bubbies, Yiddish for grandmother, only we called them Bobbi. Bobbi Balter (Hannah), my mother's mom, was my favorite. She was everyone's favorite grandma. Short, not even five feet tall, chubby, warm, and outspoken, she was respected and beloved by the whole family, except perhaps by her children's spouses. They knew not to mess with her. Outspoken to the max, she was anxiously overprotective of her children, who then passed it on to their kids and ultimately to us. She was the matriarch of the family.

Born in a small village in Kiev, she hated everything Russian, a language she knew but never spoke once she came to America. Any time the word Russia was said, she would make a spitting sound. At the age of fifteen, she traveled to America with her brother and sister, arriving to join cousins living on a farm in Peekskill, New York, around the year 1900. She married her cousin Israel and together they had four children. First they farmed, then moved to the Bronx and had a small store.

What was it like for you, Hannah Balter? I was only about fifteen when you died, so I never got to ask you that. Not that you would have told me. The only thing you told me about living in Russia was that you rode to school on a pony. How lucky can you be!

My perception of her life changed precipitously when I shared the above with my cousin Marilyn, my aunt Mimi's daughter. She recalled the years during WWII when her father was in the army overseas. She described living with her mother and grandmother in a tiny apartment in NYC. Perhaps only five years old, sitting on Bobbi's lap, Marilyn

16

remembered only one unforgettable sentence: "They came and cut the babies out of the mothers' stomachs!" No wonder our grandmother's frequent disparaging comment was, "Men are dogs," which I can recall hearing, without understanding, as, "Men and dogs!" My aunt Mimi quickly silenced her mother, and she never spoke again about Russia to any of us kids.

Mom, Bobbi Balter's daughter Esther, was born in 1914. She was the oldest child, followed by Nat, Mimi, and Joe. They all helped in the grocery store. I never knew my grandfather, Israel, as he died of blood poisoning a long time before I was born, when my mother was sixteen. Nobody in the family ever talked about him, so he remains another mystery person in my life. In fact, I never heard anybody talk about those who died, ever, especially if they were men. Hmmm.

Bobbi Balter died of a stroke before she was seventy years old, and I was fifteen. She was beloved and greatly mourned by the females in our family.

The Landaus

MORRIS LANDAU, MY FATHER'S FATHER, is a total unknown to me. He died and no one ever talked about him. Thanks to a newly found second cousin, who did some genetic research, I now know a bit about him and his family. In tracing her family tree, she discovered us!

She was told that the two brothers (our grandfathers) had had a bitter fight in the old country and immigrated separately to America to avoid being drafted into the Austrian army, which was a death sentence for Jews. The brothers never talked to each other again. I knew of no relatives on my father's side of the family until she recently wrote to me, over a hundred years after they immigrated to America!

Rose Landau was my father's mother. Bobbi Landau was also a complete mystery to me. She immigrated to the United States with her brothers between 1890 and 1900(?) from Galicia in Eastern Europe, a province that since the thirteenth century had been a war zone. Depending upon which country was the victor, Galicia was alternately part of Russia, Poland, Hungary, Austria, or the Ukraine. It didn't matter which government they were under, though. They were persecuted by them all.

Like my mother's parents, the family scraped up enough money by selling and sacrificing everything to get their children out of danger. Only their male children had a (religious) education. Rose never went to school and was illiterate. She was crippled by a fall that broke her ankle when she was a teenager after she immigrated to America. She married Morris and had two sons, my father and his younger brother Max.

Both Morris and Max died of tuberculosis when my father was about 12. He then became the sole support, provider, friend and caregiver of his mother. Totally dependent upon, and totally controlling of him.

When my parents got married in 1938, Bobbi Landau moved in with them, and this was a *disaster*. Her complaining, bullying, and bossing my mother around almost led to Mom having a nervous breakdown. (Did she really come after Mommy with a knife?) At the insistence of Mom's cousin Charlie (who was highly respected because he was a doctor) and her own mother, Bobbi Balter, my father moved his mother to her own apartment.

(Bobbi Landau on the left, Bobbi Balter on the right. This picture was taken at my brother's Bar Mitzvah, the only time I could recall seeing them together.)

Moving her meant that Dad's meager salary was split supporting his mother and us. In addition, as the dutiful son that he was, he obeyed her demands to visit her twice daily. He left early in the morning before going to work to see her. He visited her again after work, before coming home, to shop and bring her fresh milk, groceries, or whatever she wanted. Mostly she wanted *him*. The older women were the bosses in our family!

I avoided her as much as I could, only visiting her in her tiny two-room apartment in the Bronx with Dad when I had to. She was short and fat. I remember her swollen purple legs as she lay in bed, and later visiting her in the nursing home. Mom never went with us to visit her, and Bobbi Landau never came to our apartment.

Ina, Ed, and I resented her and the time she took Dad away from us. We all disliked her and only went with Dad when he insisted. I felt her bitterness, anger, fear, and loneliness, and it repelled me. She died when I was eleven. It was a relief, and I did not mourn her. We did not go to her funeral, because we were "too young." So I was told. Hmmm. Did she even have a funeral? Who would have gone besides Dad?

It has been so easy to judge them from this distance, more than sixty years later. They protected us from knowing them and the hardships that forced their immigration to the States. The anti-Semitism, the pogroms. What scared them the most? What made them leave? Oh, how I wish I could ask them about their childhoods, how they got by each day, what were their fears, their joys, their hopes and dreams. Where was *God* in their lives? Was "God" only an expression, such "oh God," said in the negative about something?

Dad

My FATHER, DAVID, WAS BORN in 1908. In addition to selling newspapers as a child, he had to learn boxing to survive the toughness of the Lower East Side. Putting himself through school at night, he graduated from the City College of New York to become an accountant.

Dad was serious, stoic, unselfish, and very opinionated (like his mother). About five foot two, with a big belly, he loved all food, especially sweets and pastries, which led to an early diagnosis of diabetes. He doted on us kids, his wife, and his mother. He was a man of few words and not as talkative as the women in our family. But he did have his opinions and was not shy about telling us what he thought about our behavior in a few short words.

From Dad I learned to love Gilbert and Sullivan operettas and classical music, especially the Russian composers. Their music played throughout the apartment whenever he was home from work. He played the violin as a child, and so did I in school. Music was an escape for him, but from what? I suspect it was the only way he could express himself.

Mom

Mom was a brown-eyed, slender brunette, with slightly wavy, shoulder-length, dark brown hair, and was about five feet tall. I can still remember seeing her honeymoon pictures with Dad at Niagara Falls, smiling for the camera, looking Hollywood pretty next to balding, roly-poly Dad. She was born in 1914. I wonder, how did he win over such a beauty?

Mom's younger years are a mystery to me too. It was a family rule not to talk about anything unpleasant, and she never broke it. Like Dad, she too was stoic in her ways, uncomplaining. Her siblings adored her and (I think) took advantage of her generosity. Not in terms of money, because we didn't have any, but in terms of her time and efforts to help them with their families.

My earliest memory of my mother was of her lying on the living room couch crying. I was about two years old, and I was trying to comfort her. I was standing next to her head, kissing and babbling baby talk to her. Eddie was in his crib nearby, also crying. I could not understand the weight of the depression she felt, but I felt it through her. As a toddler I tried to comfort her.

Mom's anxiety and depressions continued throughout her life. Despite this, she was the most unselfish person I knew, kind and forgiving, rarely complaining. Her heart was open to all. She was a strong influence in my life, as most mothers are, for better or worse. For me, it was for the better. She remains the most inspiring person in my life— Saint Esther!

Born in the Bronx

THERE WERE THREE OF US kids. Ina was five years older than I, and Eddie a year younger. Ina had many friends and was never around to play with me. Eddie was the smart one, though chubby. Ina prettier, Eddie smarter. I was a middle child in every way. I stood out in the family by being the thinnest and was reminded repeatedly by my mother and grandmothers that I was too skinny. "You have to eat to live!" they all told me throughout my childhood. If I don't, I wondered, will I die?

My best memories of those earliest years were going to the zoo with Dad, first by stroller with Eddie, and then, when I was old enough, walking with them. It was only ten minutes from home. Oh, how wondrous was the Bronx Zoo, the largest zoo in the United States! With 265 acres and almost four thousand animals, it was a new world, an alien kingdom, better than *Wild Kingdom* on TV. I couldn't stay long enough or go often enough to satisfy me.

Once inside the beautifully landscaped zoo, the trees hid the tenements and apartment houses that made up the rest of the Bronx. The honking and blaring of horns on the roadways faded away, replaced with children's high-pitched sounds of glee, laughter, and crying and parents' yelling. Sparking it all were the roars of the lions and tigers, the trumpeting of elephants, and the squawking of the parrots.

Black bears, grizzlies, and pandas! Ponds, lakes, and buildings such as the monkey, reptile, and big cat houses, and African savannas. Camels, deer, and thousands of other animals of every species in the world existed here. And birds of all kinds, flying around me in huge outdoor buildings of wire mesh.

Then on to the animal rides: elephants, camels, and ponies, high up in the air above everyone! I adored the ponies most of all. I felt their strength and power as they were docilely led by their handlers. They carried me magically through the world in my imagination for many decades. In the car, I always sat in the right rear seat so I could look out the window and imagine myself riding my horse on the sidewalk, road, or grass. No longer led, *I* was in control, galloping to keep up with the car.

When I was eight or nine, my friend Tobi and I went to the zoo every Saturday, no longer dependent on my father to take me. If we could, we would have lived there.

Revisiting the same animals every week never bored me. I was most fascinated by the black panther, the same as the one on TV, an animal friend of *Sabu of the Jungle, in the Children's Hour,* broadcast every Saturday morning. I headed for him first. Looking into his eyes, I wanted him to come up to me so that I could feel his breath and touch him. I knew that he was dangerous, but not in my fantasies. I can't explain how deeply I was drawn to him. He was more special to me than the larger lions and tigers.

I was also certain that animals could think. Even separated by windows and railings, fences and wire, when I looked into their eyes and they looked back at me, the connection felt electrical. If only I could read their minds! I knew they wished to be free. What else would they tell me? Were they happy or sad to be away from home?

I watched in awe the mounted police who patrolled the zoo. They often stopped and let us pet the giant horses. I can still feel their warm wet breath as they smelled my hands for goodies. The little hairs on their soft muzzles tickled my palms. This was my dream job! I imagined how it would be patrolling the zoo every day on horseback. There I would be, high up on top of my well-trained steed, hopefully a black one with a white mane and tail. Above all the walkers and kids, I could watch out for the bad guys. I could even have a gun!

But not only were there no women mounted police, I never even saw a female cop as a child. In the '50s there were certain jobs that only men could do and women could not. I never saw a female doctor, only nurses. Same with zoo workers, dentists, school principals, politicians, and most others in authority.

I never lost my love of horses. I drew them endlessly on scraps of paper, coloring books, and school assignments. I daydreamed of them every time I needed to escape something unpleasant, such as doctor visits with needles. When I started reading comic books, I discovered that Casper the Friendly Ghost had a pony named Nightmare. Thereafter all my horses were black with a white mane and tail. I flew away every night in my dreams. I couldn't even imagine having a horse of my own.

Our family was culturally, not religiously, Jewish. I don't doubt that the trauma they experienced in Europe was echoed in my own parents' lives by the stories they heard of life in Poland and Russia. My parents knew full well what their parents had gone through, yet they kept this secret from us, their children. However, we kids would joke about our parents being neurotic, with their overprotectiveness and anxiety. These aftereffects, I learned years later, are similar to what families of combat veterans experience due to their loved ones' trauma. They now call it secondary post-traumatic stress disorder.

We never attended nor belonged to a synagogue or temple as a family. Even when Eddie was going to Hebrew school in preparation for his bar mitzvah, we never went to temple, and I had no religious education.

We didn't keep a kosher home, but pork and shellfish were verboten, forbidden. My only taste of these were in the Chinese food I eagerly ate at the nearby restaurant we went to for birthday celebrations. Shrimp with lobster sauce! Judaism was a strong identity, not a religion to me. We did celebrate Jewish holidays, such as Passover and Chanukah, by the gathering of aunts, uncles, and cousins and, of course, eating. I can still see the huge silver-and-gold carp swimming in the bathtub, alive and fresh from the market. From there it magically became gefilte fish, served with matzo and horseradish sauce. Maybe the worship of food is another religion? I didn't know what I was missing and wouldn't find out until decades later.

We lived on the second floor of an apartment building that had about eighty other apartments and tons of kids. It was truly a small town of its own. Everybody knew everyone else. Across the street from our building was The Lawn, several acres of grass and trees where we played ball while our parents sat on their lawn chairs watching us with eagle eyes.

Home 655 Pelham Parkway, the Bronx

I didn't know our apartment was small. My father's meager earnings as an accountant had to stretch between our apartment and supporting his mother in another. Ours was two and a half rooms. It had a living room and a bedroom. My parents slept in the living room on the pullout couch that became their bed at night. I shared the bedroom with my sister and brother. The *half* room was both a kitchen and an eating area. It was not large enough to seat us all, so we ate in shifts, kids first, then adults. As I picked at my food, Mom would remind me about the poor starving kids in China.

"Eat! Eat your food! There are kids hungry in Europe and China!" Guilt, guilt, guilt.

"If you don't eat, you will get sick!" And die like little Richie next door from leukemia?

The bedroom had a dresser with a mirror, worn and secondhand, that fit between the two windows that looked out onto an elevated train a block away. The windows were always shut or had screens locked to prevent us from climbing out onto the fire escape. God forbid we go out there and fall off! The shriek and rumble of the elevated trains two blocks away and the honking car horns never bothered us. We stopped hearing them. We became immune to their thunder.

The television was the most important thing in our apartment. We'd had one since 1947. Dad was entranced by the electronics and became the go-to person when family or friends needed a TV fixer. I was mesmerized by *Howdy Doody, The Lone Ranger, Flash Gordon,* and the *Children's Hour* featuring and Sabu, the boy in *Jungle Book,* with his loyal black panther, Bagheera, at his side.

I was also a regular visitor at the local library, taking out a dozen books each week.

"You can't read all that in one week!" exclaimed the librarian.

"Oh yes I can!" I replied and did.

I consumed volumes of dog and horse books. Best sellers by Albert Payson Terhune were my favorites, and I imagined a collie like his accompanying me everywhere and every night.

Since the appendectomy and the television show *Medic,* I had been drawn to entering the medical field. I didn't understand then that the best way to conquer fear was to study what frightened you. But it was much more than just fear: the ability to heal and cure was a magical power better than turning metal to gold. I added books about nurses like Cherry Ames and Clara Barton to my library list.

I did not fear much of the real world as a child. I was tough. Only at night, in the dark, did I fear what might lurk under the bed and in the closet. The shades were drawn over the window to block out the light from the busy outside world, making the room darker. I checked under the bed and in the closet for scary beings and monsters every night, even as a teenager.

Looking back, I see those first twelve years of my life were full of wonder, joy, excitement, and love. I had a very fortunate childhood.

The Visitation

⌒

WE FINALLY MOVED FROM OUR crowded apartment to a bigger place on Andrews Avenue when I was thirteen years old. Bobbi Landau, my father's mother had died, and we were now able to afford a larger place to live.

Still in the Bronx, the apartment was on the second floor of a duplex. It was narrow, with a hallway connecting the seven rooms, one after the other, in a row: in the rear were three bedrooms, then a bathroom, kitchen, dining room, and living room. A porch in the front of the house, had another spare room that was only big enough for a small bed. I slept there for only a couple of nights as I was too frightened to be by myself so far away from the rest of the family. I joined my sister in her room at the rear of the house.

But no dogs were allowed here either. I was crushed. Tropical fish, a parakeet, and hamsters instead. Adorable, fascinating, but no replacement for my longed-for dog.

"When you get married, you can have a dog," my mother explained for the umpteenth time.

When Ina left to enter nursing school, I finally had my own room. And then it happened. One night, trying to sleep with a sore throat and fever, I saw a tall, dark, cloaked figure at the foot of my bed. He appeared to be at least six feet tall. His head was covered by the hood of his robe, hiding his face, as he stood there staring at me. Who was he? Why was he here? Where had he come from? What did he want with me? What was he going to do? He looked like the Angel of Death, the Grim Reaper. Or a scary creature from *A Christmas Carol*, like the Ghost of Christmas Future. I screamed for my mother, and he disappeared. So did the fever and sore throat.

Of course, Mom didn't see him, and she told me it was only my imagination. It wasn't, nor was it a hallucination. I could see the figure clearly in the dim evening light. Was he the being that accompanied me when I was sick or who had fueled my fears of the dark since babyhood? Was it him I was looking for under my bed and in the closet? Was I to be followed by this being all my life?

I am glad we only lived in that place for three years. I was frightened every night, though I never saw him again. I would have to wait almost sixty years to discover his identity.

I now placed an imaginary protector by my bed on the floor. He was a magnificent black panther. Big and strong, wise, loyal, and protective. I was never alone again. I couldn't have my dog, but I had him.

I Get My Dog!

NONE OF US LIKED THAT apartment in spite of it being huge. After our lease was up we moved again, this time to a nice, upscale apartment building that allowed dogs on the Grand Concourse, still in the Bronx. Hooray! I began to "hound" Mom for a puppy and I was relentless. After all, she had told me that the only reason we couldn't have one before was because it was not permitted in our previous apartments. Now defeated, she took me to the nearest pet shop and I found my long dreamed of puppy. A Beagle and just eight weeks old, he was so cute and puny I couldn't resist naming him Samson. Within twenty-four hours of bringing him home, he gifted us with a large loose and smelly poop on the carpet, that was crawling with big white worms. Ugh! Off to the vet.

We knew nothing about caring for dogs, as the vet quickly found out. The worms would be easy to get rid of, but Samson was not a boy. He was a girl, which was not acceptable to mom. She refused to consider her being spayed. So, Samson was renamed Delilah (for deceiving us), and returned to the pet shop where we received our twenty dollar refund. I had my precious, long desired dog for less than two days, and again heard from Mom, "Just wait until you get married. Then you can have a dog!" Resigned to a fate of doglessness, I could only hope for one in the future.

My sister Ina with Samson/Delilah

The '50s were a time of innocence. Other than practicing air raid drills in school, taking cover under our desks in case of a nuclear attack, it was a time of safety and freedom from worry. We could never be attacked!

Nursing School

⌒

In September 1962 I had just turned seventeen when I entered nursing school. Since I hadn't yet married the doctor/lawyer/engineer my mother had dreamed of for me, I went to school. Choosing between going to Hunter College and living at home or going to nursing school and living in a dorm was a no-brainer.

As exciting as it was living away from home and being on my own, it meant confronting my anxieties about success or failure, the new and the unfamiliar. I didn't know anyone here. I was now living in Manhattan, a fifteen-cent subway ride to freedom, away from my hovering mother in the Bronx.

The dorm on Ninety-Eighth Street was a relatively narrow and small fourteen-story building sandwiched among the larger buildings of the Mount Sinai Hospital complex between Madison Avenue and Central Park. It held the dormitory, classrooms, and infirmary. I quickly learned to navigate the maze of underground tunnels that connected it to the many hospital building, and the bountiful cafeteria where hospital staff and students ate meals.

Stress caused by the demands at school was eased, I thought, by endless noshing. Everything was new: academic subjects, living with strangers, managing my time and energy, patient care. Even if I enjoyed some of those, it was still stressful. Good stress, bad stress—all were balanced by snacking, a family tradition started from birth and encouraged by my mother.

I found nursing school difficult. I couldn't slide around and take getting good marks for granted without studying, as I had in high school. I had to work hard to keep my grades up.

First Death

IN MY FRESHMAN YEAR, I saw death for the first time.

I walked into the room, which was shared by my patient and three others. The screens around one bed were drawn, closing the view from visitors and staff, but I peeked in to see him.

"Can I come in and watch you?" I asked the nurses attending to him. They nodded. I had never seen a dead person, not even my own grandmothers.

So this is what a dead person looks like, I thought, with a mixture of horror and fascination.

He was lying in his bed as two nurses washed his body before the trip to the morgue. He was expressionless, still, and pale. He somehow didn't appear to be human anymore. I watched, mesmerized, as they dispassionately washed his body, placed it on a gurney, and wheeled him away.

"Get back to your patient!" my instructor sternly rebuked me.

After I was finished with my assignment, I went back to the nurses' station to write my notes.

The head nurse, seeing my expression, told me, "You'll get used to it. You'll harden up."

Never, I thought to myself, would I ever get used to death, pain, and suffering. I vowed I would never harden. And I didn't.

That first year in school, in addition to classes in anatomy and physiology, microbiology, and other sciences, we learned basic patient care for medical and surgical patients, such as giving baths and enemas, giving meds and shots, taking temps and blood pressures, changing dressings, and monitoring IVs.

The following two years of nursing school involved rotations in obstetrics, outpatient clinics, pediatrics, surgery, and other medical specialty areas. Some were appealing, and some were appalling. I never wanted to work in the operating room again, watching surgeons sticking knives in eyes, brains, and other body parts. Obstetrics was much better! Attending labor and delivery was a much better kind of excitement. (That's me on the left, no longer skinny. Picture was taken from the Mount Sinai Hospital School of Nursing 1965 yearbook)

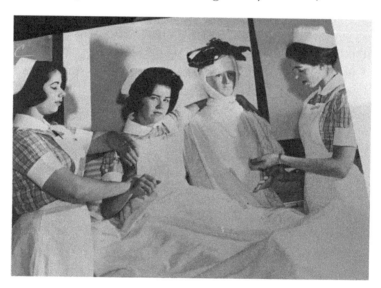

My Intro to the Mind

THE ROTATION IN PSYCHIATRY WAS a relief. It brought fascination and a lot less pressure. Classroom preparation consisted only of learning about types of psychiatric illnesses and their treatment with drugs, electro-shock therapy, and group support. *Nothing* about psychotherapy or even how to provide good listening skills.

The psychiatric unit was in one of the newer wings of the hospital and very ritzy. Getting off the elevators, you walked through a locked door into the psych ward. You had to be identified and buzzed in. You also had to be buzzed out to prevent patients from either wandering off or escaping.

From there, you could enter the large "day" room, with its huge color TV (a big deal for 1963!), card section, and comfortable chairs and couches. The walls were painted in lovely pastel shades with pictures of landscapes of natural beauty.

The patients had either private or semiprivate rooms, not like the old open wards in other parts of the hospital. They had either good in-surance or were wealthy or both.

I had no idea of the complexity and fragility of the human mind. My patients were of all backgrounds, ages, and diagnoses. Some had been diagnosed with major depression; others had psychotic disorders such as schizophrenia or bipolar disorder. They were being treated with the medications available at the time, and occasionally with ECT—electro-shock therapy.

My first assignment was "Annie." Blond, slender, and pretty, she was seventeen years old, about my age. She lived in Manhattan and attended a private school there. She had been hospitalized because of a suicide attempt.

Entering her room, I immediately spotted a picture of her and her horse. A gorgeous palomino!

"Wow! Is that your horse? He's beautiful!"

"Yeah," was her tepid answer.

"Where is he?" I asked.

"Over at the stables off the park," she answered as she waved her hand limply in the direction of Central Park.

After overdosing on pills, she had been rushed to the hospital a week ago. I couldn't even imagine how someone lucky enough to be wealthy, beautiful, and have her own horse could be depressed. I had no other background information on her. She was a mystery to me. What had precipitated her suicide attempt? I never found out.

"I don't know. I don't care." That's how she responded to my questions and attempts to get her to open up to me. Still depressed, she was difficult to engage in any conversation.

Frustrated, I couldn't connect with her at all and didn't have the skills to ask the right questions. Thankfully she had an experienced team to help her, because I couldn't.

Wandering around the unit looking for other patients to talk to, I discovered "Maddy," another Madeleine who spelled her nickname differently. A brunette like me, and about my age, but that was where our resemblance ended.

"Hi, I am Mady, I'm a student nurse here." Pretty obvious considering my uniform and name tag.

"Well, my name is *Maddy. Mady* sounds like mad, crazy."

I didn't get it. The name Mady sounded like "mad" to her, while she, Maddy, was normal? Ha! I was fascinated by her, and she could talk—nonstop, that is. About my height, she had curly, unbrushed, medium brown hair, brown eyes, and a weird, unnatural smile. Lopsided. She had been diagnosed with schizophrenia, a psychiatric condition treated with antipsychotic medication. And she was mad, meaning psychotic, though managed well enough on her medication.

"Want to know your future? I can tell you what's ahead!" she offered with a smirk.

"How can you do that?" I didn't know anything about psychics or the paranormal. As I was interested in the occult, she offered me a tarot card reading.

"Sure, go ahead," I replied eagerly as we sat down in the group room. Who wouldn't want to know the future?

"Hmmm," she said as she pulled out her tarot deck and began to read the bizarre pictures. "You are going to get pregnant and get an abortion," she pronounced with certainty and a satisfied sneer.

"What!" Oh my! was my surprised reaction.

She then tried to explain the weird pictures and how they predicted the event. Abortions weren't even legal, and I was a virgin! This was my very first experience with the occult and a "psychic." Was this real? How did she know? Was this true? Or was she just nuts?

During this rotation through psychiatry, I often wondered why the patients had been hospitalized. Why couldn't they deal with life? How did they get this way? Why would they consider killing themselves? Why and how were they so different from me? To compound the mystery, one of my classmates was admitted to the unit after I finished my rotation, and she dropped out of school. I never knew she had problems or was different from me. But then I hardly knew her.

Nursing school was tough. But I learned a profound lesson: I learned that giving relief from pain and anxiety and being a source of comfort was the best medicine, the best gift I could give to others.

I never anticipated that what I received in return would be way beyond what I gave away.

Choices to Make

⌒

I WAS PROUD TO GRADUATE from nursing school and then had some difficult decisions to make, since no one was proposing marriage. As my senior year was ending, I had to decide what to do. Should I:

1. Live at home, buy a car, and commute to work? No, no, and *no*!
2. Get my own apartment and finally get my dog? Ummm…
3. Become a nurse midwife and deliver babies in Appalachia, traveling by horseback? Really! This was 1965, and it was *actually* an option!
4. Join the military? I spent hours poring over descriptions of the roles (and uniforms) of nurses in the army, navy, and air force. I listed the pros and cons of each. The army won hands down. I wanted to go to Vietnam and work on the battlefields in what are now called MASH units. But I also knew that once I joined the military, I would not have a choice over where or how I served. So this too was a no.
5. Go back to school and get a bachelor's degree in nursing? Maybe.

Option 2 was the big winner by far!

I moved into a small apartment with a friend who first had to agree that I could have a dog. Together we went to a fashionable pet store on Madison Avenue to search for my dream dog. The puppies were all adorable and all *very* expensive. I told the saleswoman what I wanted: a Great Dane.

"Are you really prepared to give it the exercise it needs?" she asked dubiously. "My friend has one, and she drives her car with its leash attached to the door and has it run two miles every day. Can you do that?"

"Well, no," I admitted. "I don't have a car." I also had neither the time, energy, nor desire to run a few miles a day to exercise a dog and me.

"Well then, take a look at this one," she said as she returned from a room in the back.

When I saw her carrying the "more suitable" puppy, it was love at first sight! He was small, about three pounds, with a soft, fluffy coat of black, white, and brown. He was gorgeous and so adorable. I couldn't resist! I picked him up, and he smothered me in kisses.

"Only three hundred dollars!" the saleswoman said. "For another fifty dollars, you could have his even smaller brother. They are a new breed, and there are only 250 in the United States," she added, excusing their exorbitant cost.

In 1965, that was a fortune! (In today's market, $300 is about $2,500!) I gave the salesperson a check for one hundred dollars, all I had in the bank, and told her I would return with the remainder on payday. No plastic money then, thank God. Money was meaningless to me compared to puppy kisses! I was in love.

It never occurred to me then to go to the ASPCA a half a mile away and adopt a free dog who needed a home.

Tojo, my new pup, was a shih tzu, pronounced shee-zoo. More accurately, it described a *shit zoo* to me. Even though I knew all the breeds of dogs recognized by the American Kennel Club, I knew next to nothing about raising and training any of them. Tojo was a disaster in the housebreaking and furniture-chewing department. But he did keep me out of joining the army and volunteering to go to Vietnam, which I had seriously considered. Saved by a dog.

Ed

In those years I dated my share of doctors, lawyers, and engineers. I flew. I traveled to Canada, Puerto Rico, Greece, and Israel. My hunger for travel grew and has never left me. I was still single.

I had joined the Mount Sinai Hospital staff and chose to work in obstetrics, as I was dating an obstetrical resident before I graduated. That ended, but obstetrics didn't. Sinai had at that time over twelve thousand births a year. It was also a pioneer in both intrauterine transfusions and late-term abortions. Both had a strong impact on my life.

While working in the delivery room, Dr. C, one of the doctors I worked with and admired, asked me if I would be interested in helping him out in his office on alternate Saturday mornings. He was an excellent obstetrician, and, flattered to be asked, I accepted. As his office nurse, I assisted in routine tasks, such as helping during examinations and procedures.

One day a woman entered the office and said, "Hi. I'm Lucille Weiss. I have an appointment with Dr. Cherry." Pretty and slender, she was forty-seven years old and unexpectedly pregnant with her fourth child. She did not look her age!

"I should be having a grandchild, not a child," she told me half-jokingly.

"Good to see you. Dr. C will be with you in a few minutes." I just smiled and kept my mouth shut, though I agreed with her! She was Rh negative and was rightfully fearful of complications with this pregnancy.

A few weeks later, at her next appointment, perhaps to prove her point about being old enough for grandchildren, she brought with her Ed, the oldest of her three sons. He was twenty-three—and single! He was visiting from Connecticut, where he lived and worked as an engineer. At his mother's urging, he'd agreed to meet me. Are Jewish mothers telepathic?

"Go out and talk to him!" said Dr. C. "I don't need you in here."

"No! I can't leave you and her alone in the examining room!"

"Yes!" both he and Mrs. Weiss insisted. Dr. C then just about pushed me out of the room to talk to her son.

Flustered, I looked him over and found him very attractive. He had dark curly hair and was about five eight. But I didn't have time to talk. I was not supposed to leave a patient in the examining room alone with the doctor! We quickly made a date to go to the beach the next week, and I rushed back into the examining room.

The Beach

It was a beautiful August day, sunny, temperature about eighty and with a nice breeze. Perfect for a day at Jones Beach on Long Island Sound. Though it was our first date, Ed had surprised me by asking if he could bring with him his two younger brothers.

"I don't often get a chance to spend time with them," he explained. He did not see them as often as he liked, as he lived a couple of hours north in Connecticut, and they lived in New York with their mother and stepfather.

"Sure," I agreed, a bit taken aback.

And so I met Billie, age twelve, and Eric, ten. They obviously adored and looked up to their big brother. He was so kind and gentle with them. I was impressed by his attentiveness to them and their enjoyment of being with him. I watched them interact and was awed with how good he was with them. Ed was such a great big brother! A good father-to-be, too?

Together the four of us waded and swam in the ocean, then dug for clams on the beach for dinner. But no matter how much I rinsed them, they were almost inedible. Spaghetti, sauce, clams, and sand.

"Delicious! Can I have some more?" Ed gamely lied and told me what a great cook I was and swallowed the gritty meal.

When I went to work that night, after Ed and the boys had gone home, I told my coworkers, "I just met my husband." I just knew.

We continued dating regularly. Ed would come down to NYC and stay overnight at my apartment (without his brothers). Movies, restaurants, the theater. Manhattan was a great place for romance, and our time to-gether was very special. I can't say we had a lot in common at that time. He was a very practical person and I was impulsive. (Have you already guessed that?) What impressed me, then and now, was his character. What defined him as a person was his integrity, unselfishness, and hon-esty, as well as his kindness and consideration for his family and friends. In those qualities, we were a match.

Fetus or Infant?

⌒

I WALKED INTO THE ROOM prepared to monitor labor as I did every day, only this time it was going to be different. Very different. The patient was an attractive woman, hair and makeup perfectly in place, complete with lipstick and mascara, even during labor. She smiled at me when I entered and introduced myself.

Hooked up to an IV, she was waiting for her labor to be induced. Not uncommon here in the labor and delivery unit of Mount Sinai Hospital. What was different was that she was just under twenty weeks pregnant and taking advantage of newly changed New York abortion laws allowing the ending of pregnancy before twenty weeks' gestation.

This was 1966. She had just made the deadline in her pregnancy, and this was my first abortion. I was not anxious, but I was curious about what was going to happen. I was not antiabortion, remembering my tarot card reading. Who knows, I might need one myself someday.

Okay, I was cool with that. Saline solution had already been inserted into her uterus to irritate that big muscle and start contractions before I arrived. Most of my patients in labor were zonked out with heavy drugs, but she was still awake. She was not in any pain, so we could make small talk.

I sat with her, and we chatted about everything other than what was going on in that bed right now, while my right hand rested lightly on her abdomen and timed contractions.

Monitoring her labor was no different from monitoring any other patient's. Since this was the her fourth child, she went into labor quickly and easily, without pain, and surprised us both by delivering it in bed! It just slipped out with a slight push. We were both shocked.

Though it was so tiny, it was still very much alive. It squirmed and cried soundlessly as I quickly tied and cut the cord, picked it up, and wrapped a blanket around it.

I pressed the call button in the patient's room so she would not be left alone. Then I rushed it to the delivery room to suction it out and assist it in breathing. It was not a fetus to me; it was a child, a girl. She was breathing and crying, though no sounds came from her tiny mouth.

When I gently placed her on the infant scale, I found that she weighed slightly less than five hundred grams, about a pound. Her tiny body fit easily in my hands. From the delivery room, I frantically phoned the intensive care nursery unit to alert them that I was bringing them a baby, at which point the roof came crashing down on me.

"I'm bringing you a five-hundred-gram preemie that was aborted right now," I said. Mobilizing quickly, they called the labor and delivery unit to tell them what I was doing. They wanted to know what was going on.

While I was suctioning out the baby's mouth and throat and administering oxygen, the doors were noisily pushed open as doctors and nurses rushed into the room.

"Give *it* to me now!" they said as they grabbed her from me, wrapped her tightly in a blanket, then angrily kicked me out of the room, leaving her alone to die.

I was outnumbered. I left the room confused, hurt, and angry. I cried. I was devastated. I will never forget that moment. I can still feel that pain today as I write this now.

What was equally disturbing to me was the apparently callous disregard for her by the doctors and nurses who took over from me. How could they be totally oblivious to the fact that the baby could possibly survive? (It couldn't have, but I did not know that then.) They obviously did not care. What was medicine all about if not caring and healing those in need?

Did the baby have a soul? If it did, where did it go? Why did things like this happen?

I was alone with that pain. It was to be the first of future traumas that would inform and shape my life. Post-traumatic stress disorder didn't exist yet as a diagnosis. Indeed, it wouldn't be recognized for another fifteen years for those who weren't combat vets. However, I was now linked with those I would care for in the future.

Though no one would talk to me about the events of that morning, they knew enough to never assign me to another abortion patient. They also learned that they must carefully screen nurses before having them care for patients having abortions.

I am very thankful that I have never been put in the position of having to make that decision for myself. Maddy was wrong.

If I could make a wish, it would be to have sex education and birth control available for free throughout the world, to everyone in need. Prevention is the best medicine.

Would You Marry Me?

NOVEMBER WAS A HORRIBLE MONTH. I attended the births of full-term still-borns and those with awful deformities. I was in the operating room of the unit assisting in a caesarean section when I watched in horror as the obstetrician struggled to deliver a baby with an enlarged head. He had to keep cutting open the uterus wider to get it out. The baby was alive and kicking, but his future was unknown. His condition, known as hydrocephalus, had few treatments at that time, and he was rushed to the infant ICU.

Another infant that month was born with a tiny head, a microcephalic with a miniscule brain. Another I attended was born with spina bifida, a rare birth defect where the infant's spinal cord fails to develop properly due to a defect in the spine (vertebrae). A cyst forms outside the body containing spinal fluid, the spinal cord, and nerves.

To cap off the month, I was assigned a woman in labor who was heavily sedated. I timed her contractions, monitoring her and the baby's vital signs. Placing the fetoscope on her belly to listen to the baby's heartbeat, I heard something unusual: double beats! Instead of the normal 120–160 beats per minute, this was between 240 and 320 beats per minute! Worried, I hurriedly got her doctor to listen in.

"You're wrong! That heartbeat is normal," he rebuked me. "I need someone here who knows what they are doing!" He said in disgust. He then threw me out of the room. Embarrassed and ashamed, I quickly left. Another nurse was assigned to monitor her labor. But I knew what I heard!

Later that day, the doc sought me out and apologized. He told me that I was right and he was wrong. A pediatrician had been called immediately after the birth, who confirmed the abnormal heartbeat.

I thanked him, glad to be vindicated. At least that baby was treatable.

I was getting burned out fast, and I had only been on the job for a year and a half. I didn't know what else to do. I had my palm read by a psychic on Madison Avenue (no helpful answers) and bought a Ouija board. I didn't bother with tarot cards, because I thought them too weird. Also, Maddy's prediction thankfully never came true.

When Ed arrived for our next date, I got out the Ouija board before we went out to dinner. He was clearly not amused or interested.

"What is that? Why do we need it? What do you want to know?" he asked.

"When are we getting married?" I said half-jokingly.

He looked surprised to say the least, as we had not talked about the future.

"Well," he stammered, "we'll get married someday."

"Oh! That's wonderful! I am so happy!" I replied, kissing him, surprised by his answer.

"Does that mean we are engaged?"

"Uh, I guess so," he stammered.

"Great!" I exclaimed. "Can I tell my mother?"

"Uh, okay," he said, stunned. So I went right ahead and telephoned her with the good news.

"Mom, Ed and I just got engaged!" I gushed, to her surprise and delight. Poor Ed! We had been dating for less than four months.

The next day we traveled up to Rockland County, north of the city, to tell Ed's mom. She was very surprised to see us together, though she knew and was happy we were dating.

"Hi, Mom, I'm engaged," he told her.

"To whom?" she replied, confused. I didn't know that Ed also had a long-time relationship with another woman who he had been dating off and on for a few years!

"Mazol tov!" she said when she understood. And that's when she gave Ed, to give to me, her engagement ring from Ed's father her first husband. It was now official!

Understandably, Ed has never recovered from his aversion to New Age anything. He made sure I threw out the Ouija board. Oh, and Tojo had to go too. Tojo made it very clear he did not like Ed and showed it by peeing and crapping in front of him in the living room. Ed put his foot down: it was him or the dog. Not again!

Sorry, Tojo, I'm not stupid! I made sure to find him a very good, loving home. After all, Ed promised I could have another dog when we had kids. My mother was right again.

And seven months later, in 1967, Dr. C danced at our wedding.

Connecticut

WITH OUR MARRIAGE, I JOINED Ed in Connecticut. I was certain that I could eventually convince Ed to move back to Manhattan with me. I couldn't imagine not living in New York City. I got a job working in the delivery room of a small local hospital. Obstetrics was all I knew and still liked.

I loved the job but couldn't wait until we saved up enough money to buy a home and start a family. I could also then have my dog! So three years later, I retired, done with nursing and with work, when Allison was born in 1970. Jason followed a year later.

Motherhood

THE '70S WERE A DECADE of joy and pain, sprinkled with moments of ecstasy. Sort of like a vanilla-and-chocolate swirl soft-serve ice cream served with sriracha sauce sprinkled throughout.

We moved from the apartment in Southington to a house in Cheshire, Connecticut. By now I was no longer a city girl. The nice little ranch-style house on a country road was across the street from a pond, complete with serenading bullfrogs. A stream separated our property from the one next door, with an occasional visiting snake.

No sooner had we moved in than we received a nice welcome visit from two members of Temple Beth David. Did we have a sign on the door that said we were Jewish? Oh, it was probably a referral from our Jewish realtor. There were only twenty-six families that belonged to the temple, and they became our family too when we joined. We happily attended Friday night services, assorted bar and bat mitzvahs, weddings, and holidays for the first time.

Over the years, Ed and I both served on the board of directors of the temple and sent our children to Hebrew/Sunday school. I became Jewish for the first time in my life. I loved it! I also attended Torah (scripture studies), though I never learned Hebrew. I finally found out what I had been missing. My spiritual life was awakening. Taking part in Sabbath services, singing the hymns, prayers, and blessings, warmed my heart and teased my newly emerging spirituality.

During Sabbath services I noticed huge figures shining on the walls.

Were they reflections from the lamps? No, I checked that out. They were there most but not all the time. Angels? I started to ignore them. Must be my imagination.

Those first few years in Cheshire, a rural/suburban community north of New Haven, were almost idyllic. We got Sonya, a Siberian husky. The kids, toddlers then, would open the front door just to see her dash out, and they'd laugh. Lucky for us, Sonya housebroke easily and loved kids.

I felt fulfilled as a mother with Ed, and I enjoying raising two beautiful, loving children. I never missed NYC. We also got two more dogs. First Sonya the Siberian husky escape artist pictured below:

Then Tobi the bichon frise, who succeeded in eating the only rug we had in the house and all the presents under the Christmas/Hanukkah tree.

Those were wonderful years (with or without a dog). Then I screwed up, big time.

Part 2

Jewish to Christian to Cult

Weed!

IT STARTED WITH A JOINT. Here we were in our midtwenties and had never tried pot before.

"How about a smoke?" offered Hank. "Bobbie and I just bought a half ounce. We can share it."

"Are you kidding? We don't smoke," I replied, rather surprised at the offer.

"Where have you been all these years? That's unbelievable! Well then, you just have to try it! You don't know what you're missing...Pot and food, pot and sex, all great!"

Ed and I just looked at each other, then smiled and agreed to try it.

"Hmmm. Okay. Sounds wonderful, roll us a joint!" Obviously, if our good friends smoked, how bad could it be?

So we rolled a joint and smoked before making love. Then literally all hell broke out. I was transported to a scene from *Rosemary's Baby*. In hell. Only it was me and Satan, not Ed, surrounded by demons, chanting, dancing, howling, and fire all around us. In Technicolor. I was terrified, paralyzed with fear.

"Oh God, help me!" I prayed, with no relief. Then—"Adonai, Elohim, Yahweh, Jehovah, and Moses!" I called on all the Hebrew names of God and holy men I could think of. No help! Still in hell!

"Allah, Mohammed, help me," I very reluctantly prayed. Who else was there who could save me?

I finally caved in, naming in desperation the last person I could think of. "Jesus, help me!"

Instantly the nightmare/hallucination stopped, leaving me in heavenly peace, with an overwhelming sense of wonder, safety, and love. I was saved! And very confused.

I told Ed about it afterward, and he was as completely bewildered as I was. He had enjoyed the smoke and was in his own world, oblivious to me or anything else.

He looked at me in surprise. "Nope. It was great!" Another weird Mady experience.

I called Hank and Bobbie the next morning and asked if they had had any strange experiences when they smoked pot. Surprised and baffled, they said no. Only me. Why just me?

But I was shattered. This was my first ontological shock. My whole life, everything I was taught and believed in, was turned upside down. My sense of God and my identity as a Jew were totally disassembled. I continued going to temple to pray and observe the holy days. I served on its board of directors, but I was changed. No one knew other than Ed, but I had a secret, the first of many, and we never smoked weed again.

⟜⟋

It took Tara to teach me what dog ownership could really be. She was a lovely, four-year-old golden retriever who needed a new home. Her family was moving and could not take her with them. I, of course, jumped at the chance to have a fully trained dog at last! Her dad cried as he left her with us and handed over her leash. I loved her immediately.

Tara was welcomed by all of us and fit in beautifully with our family. She came when called, sat, and heeled, and after one session she knew the boundaries of our one-acre lot and never left it, even when her ball rolled into the street. My dream dog! It was as if she could read my mind, and her only wish was to please me.

She could juggle three tennis balls in her mouth at once. While lying on her back, she could pick a ball out of her mouth with her paws, extend those paws over her head, and then drop and catch the ball. Repeatedly! Everyone in the house tripped over tennis balls the whole time she was with us. We lived in doggie heaven for three years until she got cancer. Thank you, Tara! What a gift you gave me.

'

Transcendental Meditation

In 1974 WE LEARNED THAT our old friends, Bob and Joanne, were having a tag sale, as they were moving to Iowa. Bob, an engineer, had worked with Ed for many years, and he was best man at our wedding. But within a few years, we stopped socializing with them, as their progressive alcoholic dive to the gutter made it very unpleasant to be around them. They were literally falling-down drunks.

I remember our last time together. We had gone out to dinner, and we watched in horror as they consumed one drink after another. Leaving the movie theater after we ate, they could not walk without our assistance.

"Bob, can we drive you home? We're worried about you!" we offered.

"Nope, we're fine!" he replied, offended by our suggestion, his speech slurred. Joanne was no less drunk. How could they get home safely?

They made it back, but that was the end of our friendship. Having *a* glass of wine or beer was our idea of drinking. Not theirs.

A few years later we got a call from Bob out of the blue. "Come on over! We are moving and have to get rid of lots of stuff! Come say good-bye to me and Joanne and see if there is anything you want."

"You bet! What's up? How are you doing?" I asked a gazillion more questions.

We were delighted to see them now clean and sober. We bought some items and listened with fascination to their story of newfound success in life, which they attributed completely to learning to meditate. Meditate? At least *I* was fascinated. It went completely over Ed's head.

"Well, we finally realized we had a drinking problem and needed to stop. Bob got into a horrible auto accident and thank God he didn't kill anyone. That was a big wakeup call," Joanne said with a sigh. "We looked around, and AA failed us, or rather we should say we failed it. Then we heard about Transcendental Meditation. Bob's brother swore by it. Said it saved his life!"

As they invited us in for dinner, they told us more about their desperation to change their lives. Their kids were unhappy. Bob's job was tanking. They heard that TM (Transcendental Meditation) could do miracles and help them to stop drinking. So, with nothing to lose, they were initiated and started meditating twice a day for twenty minutes. Incredible!

"We don't ever need to drink again, or smoke or take drugs. Nothing is as good as meditation," they announced. "That's all we need! TM is so great. Once we got started, we couldn't wait to take more courses, and it kept getting better and better! Even the kids are meditating and loving it." On and on they went about how wonderful their lives were now and how TM had improved their relationship with each other and their kids. They also described the new TM "flying" course, "meditate and levitate," that they said they couldn't wait to take. Wow! Another of my oldest wishes!

When they were offered an opportunity to join the TM organization and teach TM and work at Maharishi University in Iowa, they decided to sell their home and move.

"You gotta try it, it will absolutely change your lives!" Hmmm…I was *very* impressed by their total change back into regular human beings, back to the friends I had gotten to know and love when I first met them eight years ago.

My First Cult

A FEW MONTHS LATER, I found a lump in my breast, and true to family tradition, I immediately started catastrophizing. An acquaintance, a member of our synagogue, still in her twenties, had just died of breast cancer last year.

"I'm gonna die!" I thought as I vividly imagined my dying and death, wondering what I would put on my tombstone. I quickly made an appointment with my doctor, who also felt the lump and sent me for tests. This was now becoming horrifyingly real.

First the ultrasound, then the needle biopsy.

"It's only a cyst. It's not malignant," the doctor shared with me afterward, to my great relief. I then remembered Bob and Joanne's revelations. I realized that now that I had a new chance in life, I too wanted the happiness and enlightenment they seemed to glow with. I began looking for a TM center. It was not hard to find; there was a TM center right there in Cheshire, Connecticut.

Now that I had made up my mind, I dropped into the center, paid my $150, and made a date for my own private instruction, which was scheduled only two days later.

In front of an elaborate Hindu altar, I was initiated with my very own special mantra designed specifically for my own unique needs. I was assured that TM is not a religion or spiritual practice. However, I learned years later that there are only eight mantras used for the entire population of meditators, all of which are names of Hindu gods and goddesses to invoke and pray to. Not so unique after all. And how is that not a religion?

It was so easy. I learned the simple steps to meditate. First I was to sit in a quiet place at home, in a comfy chair where I wouldn't be disturbed, close my eyes, breathe deeply, and repeat my *very* special, *secret* mantra, "Shring." (There! I am sharing it with you for free!) Only twenty minutes, twice a day. Easy peasy. Maybe Shring herself was helping.

On the third day of meditating, I had a life-changing experience.

After meditating for a few minutes, I relaxed and then was overwhelmed by a power I'd had no idea existed. My whole being was engulfed and swallowed up by a universe of intensely bright and glowing presence. I had never felt such unconditional, overpowering love. I entered and was lost within. Then the tears began to flow. This was my second ontological shock after the marijuana only a few short months before.

I couldn't wait to get back to the TM center for my next "lesson." I eagerly explained my experience and wanted to know what had happened to me. My instructor looked away and simply stated that I was "unstressing." No big deal. Unstressing? The most mind-expanding, beautiful moment of my life was a big *nothing*? He suggested I take a course on the science of creative intelligence, which would explain more.

I quickly signed up and took it, but it didn't explain anything. Just another $150 wasted. It was just a preamble for more and more courses. And more and more dollars. The goal, I was told, was to attain "cosmic consciousness, an awareness of everything."

"The best way to do this is to join the staff of TM and become a Governor of the State of Enlightenment," they eagerly encouraged me, like my friends Bob and Joanne. "At the same time, you could learn how to fly!"

Now here are my two earliest wishes, from age seven: to expand my consciousness and know everything, as well as be able to fly. I then watched a video of TMers bouncing on a mat as they were "levitating." They did not remain suspended in the air for even one second. This didn't look like anything I had longed to do, but maybe it was a beginning. The only drawback was that I would have to leave my family for the three-month course. No can do. Three months to just bounce on a mat?

I started looking for something that would explain my profound experience in meditation. I knew it was much more than unstressing. It was *cosmic.* I could not accept that this was simply a brain dump and that I would have to spend many months away from my family, and thousands of dollars, to achieve higher states of consciousness. Wasn't my experience already a higher state of consciousness? I asked our rabbi about this, and he didn't have a clue.

Fortunately, one of the first books I came across in my search for an answer was William James's *The Varieties of Religious Experience.* His description of mystical states put into words what I couldn't describe myself. It was much more than an aha moment. I immediately related to the word that he used to describe this indelible feeling: bliss. I was relieved that I wasn't crazy and had not just unstressed. I hungered for more. In addition, his book *predated* TM by sixty or seventy years. He obviously knew more than they did. I could now search for spiritual growth outside of TM as well.

The search began, and I consumed books on Buddhism, Hinduism, Sufism, and the mystical elements of Catholicism. The works of Thomas Merton, Pir Inayat Khan, Idries Shah, Thich Nhat Hanh, and many others were scattered around my spare room. Many paths to the one goal. Since I didn't know Hebrew, I skipped the Kabbalah, the mystical side of Judaism.

I also started reading everything I could get my hands on about psychic phenomena, such as remote viewing, telepathy, astral projection, and reincarnation. I sought out books by Edgar Cayce, Charles Tart, and Russell Targ. My crystal collection began to grow.

First Hypnotic Regression

SINCE ALTERED STATES WERE FASCINATING to me, I went to a lecture on hypnosis and eagerly listened to stories of past-life regressions. When the speaker asked for a volunteer from the audience, there I was in the front row, almost leaping out of my seat, waving my hand madly in front of his face. Me! He had no choice but to choose me!

I sat down on the stage in a comfy chair, closed my eyes, and went into a trance.

"Close your eyes and breathe deeply. Inhale through your nose, and exhale through your mouth," he instructed. "Now relax your face, then your shoulders…" He had me relax all the way to my toes. "Now, going deeper and deeper, see the door ahead, and open it."

I stepped through it as he suggested and then looked down at my feet as he commanded.

"Describe what you see."

"They're brown and dirty. I'm barefoot," I said as I stared at them, not believing what I was seeing.

"Describe yourself now. What are you wearing?"

Hesitating, I related, "I am dressed in rags or something primitive. I am young, maybe six years old."

"See yourself older until you see something different," he then commanded.

"I am living in a hut or some kind of primitive dwelling. I am now a young teen, maybe fifteen, and I have a little baby. We're hungry. I'm scared and sad and sick," I complained. I assumed I must have died shortly afterward, because that was all the hypnotist wanted to hear from me.

He brought me out of trance with a look of disappointment and disgust. I guess I had failed in some way, as that lifetime wasn't what he had in mind for entertainment. I too was disappointed. I would have chosen anything more interesting or important if I could have. A queen, a famous writer or actress? But maybe that was the only "past lifetime" I had.

The American Red Cross

⌣‿⌐

COLLEGE WAS BEGINNING TO LOOK good again. The kids were starting school, and I had too much time on my hands. I knew I didn't want to go back to bedside nursing. I started to think about becoming a nurse midwife. That meant a bachelor's and then a master's degree in nursing.

Taking it slowly, I enrolled in a local community college and took a few courses. Surprise! I got all A's. I gained in confidence and applied and was accepted to the University of Massachusetts's University Without Walls. I could then attend classes and do independent studies to get the rest of my bachelor's degree. But not in nursing. I had a choice. I could accept sixty credits toward any bachelor's degree, but only thirty-two if I wanted it in nursing. I would have to repeat courses in nursing that I already took years ago, such anatomy, physiology, and microbiology. I would also have to travel. That meant three hours of commuting from my home in Connecticut to Amherst, Massachusetts, a few times a week for classes.

After much thought and discussion with Ed, I chose to get my bachelor's degree in human services administration. Together with the sixty credits from nursing school and thirty more from local college courses, I could receive my BA in another year.

At the same time, I knew it was time to go back to work. It was now 1977. The kids were in school all day, and I was bored. I found a job at the Hartford chapter of the American Red Cross. I had been a volunteer in their blood program, staffing bloodmobiles for several years, and therefore had a great background when applying for the position of assistant director of the blood program. I had now left bedside nursing for good. My job was to arrange for and "sell" companies into sponsoring bloodmobiles, as the Red Cross was the only nonprofit agency in Connecticut tasked to provide hospitals with a blood supply.

Father Ted: Intro to Catholicism

DRIVING INTO THE PARKING LOT at work that first day, I found a space behind a brand-new Datsun 280Z. I must admit, I was somewhat of a snob, so I parked my Porsche right next to it.

The Porsche itself had a story. Looking for a used car, I saw an ad in the paper for a reclaimed stolen 1972 Porsche 911. Allstate was going to sell it to the highest sealed bid. Meditating on a number, I added fifty dollars to the amount that came to me, as I didn't have much confidence in my "psychic ability." I bid $3,250 for the car and won it, sixty dollars higher than the next highest bid. I could have gotten it for ten dollars over the next highest bid if I had trusted my "psychic" ability. Oh, if only I could do that with lottery numbers.

Upstairs in the office, Chase (Charles) Sanborn—not the coffee—confidently introduced himself, pointing out his new Datsun Z. I countered with, "Oh yes, and that's my Porsche." That was a very big mistake. Chase, a social worker in the next office, was working with the ARC services to military families. He did not like to be, or have, the second best of anything. More about him later.

Also, that first month on the job, I bumped into a Catholic priest.

"Hello, I am Father Ted," he said. "I volunteer here on Mondays."

"Hi," I said, startled. "I never met a priest before!" I blurted, to my embarrassment.

We were both surprised by my outburst and laughed, so we made a beeline to the coffee pot and started talking. We instantly became friends. He was about my age, skinny, with brown hair and a mustache. He was also energetic and interesting. I told him I that I had never talked to or even met a priest before, and of course, I had never been to a Mass.

"Well, that's easy to fix! How about coming to Mass with me, then joining me for lunch in the rectory?"

Ted and I continued to meet a couple of times a month for Mass and lunch. We also went to the beach and took long walks. Until then, I had felt an almost knee-jerk revulsion for anything Christian, *especially* Catholicism.

Sacred Heart Church was in the middle of a Spanish-speaking, mostly Puerto Rican neighborhood in Hartford, and the Mass was in Spanish. Somehow that made it easier and less foreign. I had spent vacations in Puerto Rico with friends and spoke some Spanish. The church itself, built in 1917, was magnificent with its stained-glass windows and ornate woodwork. I was enchanted, and I was very drawn to the Eucharist.

Ted was the first and only person with whom I could discuss religion and mysticism. I then devoured the works of Thomas Merton, Dietrich Bonhoeffer, Henri Nouwen, and others that he recommended.

One day I said, "Ted, I have been giving this a lot of thought, and I wanted to tell you I want to convert to Catholicism."

"*What?* Are you kidding me?" I thought he was going to faint when I told him.

Being a Jew, my distrust of and aversion to the Catholic Church and Christianity were rooted in the history of the Spanish Inquisition, the centuries of persecution, anti-Semitism, and finally the Holocaust. But the pull of the Eucharist overcame everything, I explained.

In the months that I attended Mass, I had watched as others lined up to receive the host and the blessings, with an increasing hunger for the Eucharist. I could not ignore my experience of Jesus a few years before when smoking pot. I strongly felt that I was led to be here. Since I couldn't attend the formal RCIA (Rite of Christian Initiation of Adults) classes at the church, as they were taught in Spanish, our lunchtimes at the rectory became our classroom.

I also told Ed. I can't say that he ever understood *why* I was doing this, but he also did not strongly object. Mostly he was silent. I shared with him what I was feeling, and he knew of my experience of being "saved" by Jesus a few years ago. We agreed not to reveal this immediately to friends and family. I am sure he was hoping this phase would pass as quickly as others had!

I asked Ted to be my godfather, and he administered the rites of baptism and first Communion. I asked a good friend from work to be my godmother. It was a noon Mass on a weekday and was only sparsely attended. It felt like we were the only worshippers present and had that beautiful church to ourselves.

During the baptism, and while receiving the Eucharist, I felt transported to a world of transcendent peace, love, and beauty.

I made a deal with myself to attend church and Mass for one year and see how I felt in this strange Christian community. I wanted to experience all the events of the Church calendar. My relationship with God and Jesus felt strong and beautiful, but the physical church? Catholicism? That was something else. The history of the Church appalled me, and I needed to separate the religion somehow from the physical church.

A year after I met him, Ted was transferred to another parish. I attended Mass for another few months in different churches and communities until I gave up trying to find a comfortable place to worship. I felt done with Catholicism. I just didn't feel comfortable in *any* church. My family and friends knew by this time that I had converted, and they thought me beyond nuts. It wasn't the first time and wouldn't be the last time they thought that. Perhaps they were right.

Into the New Age

I NOT ONLY READ ABOUT but began to experience some weird events. It was easy for me to get into a trance and go from meditating to searching. Remote viewing looked like almost as much fun as I imagined flying to be. I read all I could find about it. Books by Charles Tart, Dean Radin, and others stretched my imagination, and I began to try out their exercises.

The first time I tried to experience remote viewing, I closed my eyes and looked to see where my mother was that day. I then "saw" her at Lennox Hill Hospital with her sister, visiting someone there. Coming out of trance, I immediately called her.

"Mom, were you with Mimi this morning at the hospital?" I asked. I described where she was and what they were wearing. Well, it freaked her out when I told her what I saw!

"How did you know? What are you doing?"

I quickly stopped talking when she confirmed what I had seen and I heard her distress on the phone. She could not comprehend what I was saying.

Later, I tried it again, "seeing" Chase (remember the guy with the Datsun?) with his girlfriend in their backyard. When I told him, he sternly rebuked me for spying on him, saying, "Don't you *ever* do that again!"

I immediately stopped doing any remote viewing. It was obviously not having a good effect on those I checked on.

I also found that I began to be aware of strong, unpleasant feelings arising from loved ones within my family who lived at a distance. Maybe I wasn't seeing them, but I began *feeling* them, especially their anger and anxiety.

While at work, for the first time in my life, I had a severe anxiety attack. It was horrible. All I knew was that something awful was either happening or going to happen. My heart was racing, and I couldn't pay attention to anything or anyone.

I called my mother as soon as I got home. "Mom, are you okay?"

"Mimi is in the hospital," she told me anxiously. "She had a nervous breakdown. They took her by ambulance and she needed ECT—electro-shock therapy."

From then on, when and if I ever felt any overwhelming negative emotions, I checked with my family, especially my mother and sister. But first, I needed to learn to distinguish if they were *my* feelings or the feelings of another. That was very difficult for me, as my life was now feeling like a roller-coaster ride.

Deaths and Ghosts

WHEN MY FATHER WAS DIAGNOSED with cancer, over the course of several months, he was hospitalized for surgery, then went to a rehabilitation facility for several weeks, and then requested to go home to die. He was home for about a week when, while I was at work, I suddenly knew he was about to die. Soon! I just knew it! I called my mother.

"Mom, I'm coming home now. How's Dad?" I double-checked.

"Well, he is not doing so good. He's sleeping a lot and talking to his mother."

I abruptly left work that morning after calling Ed and took the Amtrak train to NYC and a cab to their apartment in the Bronx.

After the four-hour trip, I discovered I had arrived just an hour too late. He had already died. I sadly said goodbye to him as he lay in his bed. At least I was able to spend some quiet time alone with him before they took him to the funeral home.

Mom told me that before he died, he was speaking to his mother, whom he "saw" and "heard" in the room. She had died twenty years ago! Of course, we assumed he was hallucinating. I was just glad he was at peace and no longer suffering.

A few months later we visited Hattie, Ed's grandmother, in her hospital room in New York. She was dying of breast cancer. But she was hanging on, afraid of dying and what was to come. We visited and told her we loved her. Remembering my father talking to his mother and then dying shortly afterward, I gently said to her, "Did you know that Jules is waiting for you with a big lobster?" Jules, her husband, had died a few years previously.

"You really think so?" she said hopefully and smiled a little. Hattie, we learned, passed peacefully that night.

Not long afterward, a young woman came up to me at a party. "There's an elderly woman who wants to thank you," she said.

"Who?" I asked.

"I don't know who she is, but she recently passed," she replied, looking puzzled.

We chatted a bit and became friends. Her name was Georgia. I had never met anyone who was really psychic before. All the others were clearly faking. Georgia told me that she didn't know the circumstances of the thank you, just that she needed to tell me that. Was that Grandma Hattie?

Working down the hall from me at the Red Cross was Marilyn, a lovely social worker. Though I didn't know her well, I never suspected she was troubled or depressed. One morning I was stunned to hear that she had committed suicide the night before by sitting in her closed garage with her car running. Everyone at the office attended her funeral, along with her family and friends. During the memorial, I saw a large dark cloud float above the congregation and depart out the window. I poked the person next to me, but no one else saw it. I looked around to see if anybody was smoking a big cigar. Nope. Was that her spirit? Could we really exist apart from our body? And why did I alone see her?

Chase

BACK TO CHASE—CHARLES WALTER SANBORN Jr. He was four years younger than I, about five ten, olive complexioned, and skinny. Not bad looking, kind of cute. He was very intense, with curly brown hair and green eyes that stared right through you. We became friends, and with him being single, I immediately began playing matchmaker, fixing him up with my single girlfriends.

Chase had spent a lot of time in Marilyn's office. I once asked him if he had ever dated her, and he looked surprised and said, "Absolutely not! She's married, and I avoid married women like the plague. I don't need an angry husband coming after me with a shotgun!"

I don't know that I truly believed that, but her death ended any speculation.

I then thought of Georgia, who I felt sure would be a great match for Chase. He agreed to meet her, and I arranged to have us get together for lunch at a restaurant near our office at the Red Cross. It seemed a good match, and when the conversation turned to the subject of reincarnation and past lives, Georgia and I eagerly agreed to have Chase regress us right then and there.

The noise level at that loud and busy restaurant was no problem. Chase put both Georgia and me quickly into a light trance and regressed us to another lifetime. I found myself as a woman in South America during a time of civil unrest, and I met Chase there! I do not recall much else of what happened, but I was impressed that I even recalled that much.

I left them at the restaurant for some privacy and went back to work. I was glad to know there was more to my past lives than just a starving girl in a primitive past. It didn't bother me that I couldn't recall much of that session. Too bad.

I tried to reach Georgia later to find out how her date with Chase went. "How did it go with Chase? Did you have a good time?" I asked.

"Don't you *ever* call me. I never want to speak with you again!" she replied angrily and hung up.

Confused, I asked Chase what had happened, and he just glared silently at me. His eyes bored into mine, and he looked angry. I never questioned him again about it, and I never tried to fix him up again either.

What the hell had happened?

A month or so later, I thought it would be great if Chase hypnotized me for weight loss. He was obviously quite good at it. We quickly agreed on a price and time. He was a friend and coworker, and I trusted him. We went to the house of one of his friends, and at his suggestion, I lay down upon the bed and went into trance quickly at his direction. Being a meditator, I was now very familiar with altered states, and he had already been able to hypnotize me before at dinner in a busy restaurant.

Coming out of trance, I had absolutely *no* recall about what had happened during that session. However, I was pleased to quickly lose the twenty-five pounds I couldn't get rid of on my own.

During the ten years that I knew Chase, I was at my chosen, ideal weight. I would not find out what his other suggestions to me under hypnosis were until after that.

When I graduated from UMass, I wondered what to do next. I inquired at Yale University about their midwifery program, but I was not eligible, as my bachelor's degree was in human services, not nursing. Okay, I thought, what else can I do? Go back to UMass?

I had already been invited by one of my professors to continue my education at UMass and get my doctorate in psychology there. I was flattered, but it would have been difficult going to classes in Amherst while living, working, and raising two kids in Connecticut, and I declined that opportunity.

Chase was entering a master's program in counseling at Central Connecticut State College and suggested we get our counseling degrees together. Hmmm.

All it took was a suggestion by Chase to quickly make up my mind. It never occurred to me that all "my" decisions were not really "mine."

We began the master's program at Central, and Chase, who already had a bachelor's degree in social work, opened his office in Hartford. The plan was for me to join him as a counselor when I finished my degree.

Some interesting things happened in and out of my classes, some of which I took with Chase. In Marriage and Family counseling, our professor asked, "Who knows what you can do when the couple complains of—"

I raised my hand. "Uh…uh…" I opened my mouth to offer my suggestions, but no sound came out. I was in a panic. My mind was completely blank, empty! No thoughts at all! Alarmed, I looked around wildly, then over at Chase, and I saw him covering his mouth, obviously laughing.

Another time, as we were crossing the street by the office, I tripped over nothing. Picking myself up, I saw him again laughing. I began to suspect, but couldn't understand how, that he had some control over me.

I also saw him walk through a wall. Impossible! When I excitedly told him what I saw, he just smiled at me and said nothing. I also believed he could read my mind and play my emotions like a guitar. One moment I'd be happy and smiling, the next in tears, all by how he talked to or looked at me or ignored me. I learned that if he was displeased by anything I did or said, it meant being ignored. The worst punishment. He was becoming my guru, a god-man.

After Chase met Emma, a lovely woman from Puerto Rico, the four of us became good friends, and Ed and I danced at their wedding. They maintained homes both in Connecticut and on the island, and we sometimes vacationed there with them during the winter. We all bought ATVs and sped around the Connecticut River trails and open spaces. We had lots of fun together.

As we became closer, the four of us entered a real estate partnership, buying and restoring damaged, older homes. We refinanced our house and used the equity for investment. The four of us worked together, painting, tiling, carpeting, and upgrading the homes for resale. Some of the multifamily properties we kept for rentals. A lot of work, a lot of fun, but the profit was questionable. I collected the rents and handed them over to Chase, who paid the mortgages and expenses.

Partnership with My Guru

⟶

In 1979, Chase and I both got our master's degrees in counseling, and I joined him in his office on Pratt Street in downtown Hartford. It was an older building, and our furnishings were secondhand. I did all the billing (and cleaning) as I slowly built up my own caseload.

Chase's client load was already increasing rapidly. He was very charismatic, and his clients, both men and women, loved him. They referred their friends and family to this infinitely wise person until his caseload was full. Those he couldn't, or more likely didn't want to see, were referred to me and another friend of his, Betty, who joined the practice as well for a short time.

We offered counseling sessions on a sliding scale, and most of our clients paid the minimum. We were not eligible to charge our clients' insurance policies, and therefore they paid out of pocket for their sessions.

Chase hinted at mysterious, secretive work he was doing for the government. He did say that the covert work had begun when he was in the army in Vietnam. He would disappear for weeks at a time now to do this "work." One day, an official government letter came to our office addressed to a Major Charles Sanborn. He quickly took it from me and said nothing. An officer! That confirmed he must be telling the truth. My respect for and wonder at him deepened.

I learned more about him over the years. He was the oldest of three sons. His father, he said, was an alcoholic and physically abusive. He described his youngest brother, Michael, dismissively as a mama's boy, and his middle brother, Jack, as a psychopath and a member of a dangerous street gang. When Jack stopped by our office one day, Chase introduced me as an expert in kung fu, a giant exaggeration. I didn't know then that he was afraid of Jack.

In fact, when I began taking kung fu, Chase didn't like that either. I don't recall telling him about it or hearing him say that he didn't want me to learn it. I just knew. I switched to tai chi. Was he afraid of me too?

As our psychotherapy practice became more successful, he invited me to be his partner. All I had to do was convince Ed that his retirement savings from his job would be a good investment. Sounded like a great idea. Our practice was growing and steady. Ed readily agreed. Charles Sanborn and Associates. I was listed as an associate. Hmmm. I know I raised questions about the name of our "partnership," but I have no memory at all of the discussion other than knowing it changed nothing.

Ed and I were now ready for another dog. We missed Tara, and I wanted a *big* dog! I mentioned to Chase that we were thinking of an English mastiff. Looking at me sternly, he said that that was a poor choice and we would be sorry if we got one. So Ed and I waited and didn't get any dog. At least for a while.

I also took courses in neuro-linguistic programming (NLP). I wanted to learn additional therapeutic modalities, especially hypnotherapy. The weekend courses throughout the year were very entertaining, to say the least.

NLP's originators, Richard Bandler and John Grinder, with their spouses, would begin the lectures by putting us students in trance. I was a great subject. Now, thirty-five years later, I still remember their assurances that you cannot make someone do something through hypnosis against their will. Wrong! I will explain why later, in the next chapter.

Chase did not approve of me taking NLP and belittled the training, but I had already signed up and paid for it. After I began the course, I learned some cool techniques of hypnotic induction, which, ironically, I did not recognize were being used against me by him on a regular basis. I learned how to induce a hypnotic trance simply by altering the tone and cadence of my voice, by using light touch on an arm and guided imagery, and much more.

When I thought NLP could be helpful to my clients therapeutically, I always talked to them and educated them about what it might be able to accomplish as far as their goals were concerned. I always asked permission before inducing a trance. I assumed Chase did this as well. Nope!

Dr. Mady and Dr. Chase

I HAD THE OPPORTUNITY, THROUGH the American Nurses Association, to become a Clinical Specialist in Adult Psychiatric and Mental Health Nursing in 1981. Chase and I had been in practice together about two years. With this change in the nursing profession, I did not need a bachelor's or master's degree in nursing but could be grandfathered into this new clinical category by taking and passing extensive (and difficult) exams. My RN and master's degree in counseling would be enough to make me eligible.

I took the preparatory courses and passed the examination. Now I was Madeleine Tobias, MS, RN, CS! This change made our client visits eligible for insurance reimbursements, and our income went up significantly.

My degrees were now "better" than Chase's. I knew he did not like me having any professional edge over him, but he liked the additional money that came in. It also made me less dependent upon him, as I could now, if I wished, leave the practice.

It soon became apparent he thought that if he got his doctorate, he would be superior to me. He began researching fast and easy ways to get his degree. Finally, he found Heed University, then located in Florida. To earn a PsyD, a doctorate in psychology, all you needed to do was pay them $3,000 and earn eighty credits, twenty of which were earned by the dissertation, and you could earn up to sixty credits for life experience!

In the 1970s and '80s, distance learning schools were springing up. Heed, in addition to Walden University, the Union Institute, Nova, and others, offered a variety of master's and doctoral programs that offered noncampus courses. Some of these nontraditional schools then went on to become affiliated with universities and became legitimized. Heed, though, never became legitimized or accredited and dropped the doctoral programs years later.

Recalling that *I* still had a possibility of finishing up my doctorate at UMass, Chase quickly suggested we both get our degrees together in a fast, cheap, and easy way. I was beyond questioning him at this point. I wrote my dissertation on eating disorders. After all, I had a great background in food.

After we finished our dissertations, we both obtained our doctorates almost immediately. I didn't learn until much later that one of his client/lovers wrote his dissertation for him, and he had to go to the university and defend it. He stated that *he* had to go to Heed to defend *mine*, and he said I should be grateful to him!

Why did we need doctorates? I think he just enjoyed being called Dr. Sanborn and that I was then no longer professionally superior to him. He had to be at the top and the center of attention, *always*. In addition, he knew I might decide to go back to UMass and actually get a real doctorate, which I had been encouraged to do.

In the mid-'80s, Chase divorced Emma, and his new girlfriend, Cathy, and her two girls moved into his spacious home, complete with indoor pool. Shortly before his divorce, which I didn't know was coming, he asked me to park $250,000 in our office account. Afterward I learned that he needed to hide the money from his wife for the divorce settlement. He trusted me implicitly.

Up to this point, he was almost godlike to me. He had told me early in our relationship that he was a disciple of Sant Darshan Singh, of the Radhasoami mystical tradition. I knew other followers of this group, including a sociology professor of ours at Central Connecticut State College. This added to its respectability. He hinted that he had left the group because he no longer needed it. Was he now a guru?

I witnessed what I believed were supernormal powers. Chase could walk through walls, was an incredibly good psychotherapist, and could read my and other people's minds. When I was suffering from low-grade fevers for several weeks, he told me that my temperature would return to normal if I got off my vegetarian diet and started to eat meat again. It worked! I adored him and his wisdom.

I was a loyal lieutenant to this general. I was trustworthy to the max. I ran our various businesses, paid the bills, managed clients' affairs. No, not love affairs; I mean schedules and payments. And worst of all, I collected outstanding bills for the both of us.

He was my guru. And when I began to have doubts about him, I just put them on a tall shelf at the back of my mental closet.

The Shelf Is Cracking

DURING OUR REAL ESTATE BUSINESS, Chase's girlfriend, Cathy, worked at a mortgage company. Shortly after they became lovers, she and Chase opened their own mortgage company. Chase invited me and other friends to join them, and I learned how to sell and write mortgages. I also continued to manage our psychotherapy practice and collect the rents on our properties.

However, things just started to smell. I made a lot of money that year. I was a good salesperson and was very convincing when I believed that a product or service would benefit others. However, I was being pressured by Chase and Cathy to slip in an added point to the closing fees. A point was 1 percent of the amount of the mortgage. If you borrowed $200,000 to buy your house, that would be an additional $2,000 at closing added to the cost of the mortgage. The mortgage salesperson would get 50 percent of the point as a bonus. I did that just once and then felt so awful, I never did it again and left the company. But not the psychotherapy practice.

How did I rationalize his behavior to myself? During the years with Chase, I had to juggle the good with the increasingly bad. His clients, both male and female, adored him. Some of the men gave him money to invest, and undoubtedly some of the women slept with him. But I tried not to think of or believe either of those things.

The weight of those doubts began putting deeper cracks on the shelf. Symbolically, it was at that point that we got another dog, an

English mastiff. Jesse was a wonderful dog, 150 pounds, loyal and gentle. I ignored Chase's suggestion/order for the first time. I then rescued Pipsqueak, 185 pounds. I couldn't have enough really big dogs. This is a picture of Jesse and Pipsqueak, with my daughter Allison and myself.

When I quit the mortgage company, I was doing an emotional juggling act. I was a witness to Chase's greed, selfishness, and profound disregard for others. The game he was playing with my life was ending. But how would it end? There was so much invested in our partnership, my career, and even my relationship with Ed. I was immobilized by fear. Dread. I couldn't come to terms with the two opposing truths I had been living with. He was either a brilliant spiritual person, my personal guru, or he was a sociopath.

Another old friend of Chase's also joined his mortgage company briefly and left. Fred had known Chase since high school and started telling me stories about their childhood and adolescence. One day over coffee, he shared that Chase got into trouble in high school when he got drunk and wrecked his and another's car.

"Nobody died, but he was arrested and given the choice of either going to jail or joining the army."

"So that is how he got to Vietnam?" I asked.

"No! No, he never went to Vietnam. He was stationed in Germany the whole time."

So much for the war hero, I thought. All lies.

I had no problem leaving the mortgage company provided I continued in the psychotherapy practice. When I had first joined the practice, I signed a noncompete clause that stated if I left, I could not continue seeing any of our clients, nor could I work within fifty miles of the office. I had thought that was a nonissue at the time, but not now.

In addition, Ed and I had thousands of dollars invested in the houses we'd bought and refinished with Chase that were not sold yet. That was going to be a nightmare of its own. I was stuck. The shelf had broken, but I was not free.

I was truly relieved in 1987, when Chase told me he was going to move to Florida and "retire"—in less than two weeks!

"You're leaving? Why?" I asked.

He just glared at me, not speaking. Silly me. I should have known I wouldn't get an explanation.

Together we told his group, and he informed his other clients. He was their beloved therapist and friend. They grieved their loss, said their goodbyes, and showered him with gifts. Some of them had been seeing him for eight to ten years and were distraught. No explanation, he just wanted to move on.

I inherited his group and some of his individual clients. None in the group left. They knew me well, as I covered for Chase on his frequent vacations and then winters in Puerto Rico. I was their sole link to him. If they were relieved that he left as well, they did not disclose it.

By that time, we had sold our remaining properties, and the financial reality of how he had swindled us in our investments became clear. Much too late.

He left, but not with Cathy. She called me at home early one morning. In tears, and with much anger, she told me what was happening.

"He's gone! He dumped me! He said he's tired of the relationship and it just wasn't working!"

"What? What about your business, the kids?" I was boggled by the news.

"That's just the problem! When I told the kids about it, they were sooo happy! Then it came out that he was abusing them. I think he was making a quick exit because he was afraid they would tell me and I would send the police after him!"

"Well, are you going to do that? He deserves to go to jail!" I replied angrily.

"No! I am afraid of him going after us! I'm scared of him hurting me or the kids."

Her two beautiful young daughters, six and eight years old, despite their fear of him, finally revealed to Cathy that Chase had been sexually abusing them. He had bullied them and threatened them if they told their mother.

That would explain his "Hi, I am leaving" and sudden disappearance!

Stunned and horrified, my rage at ten years of deception and emotional abuse erupted and overflowed. Knowing he liked to sleep late, I called and woke him up, seething.

"Never, ever talk to me again," I said, then hung up on him before he could respond. We never spoke again.

No wonder he was leaving—and leaving with Ruth, a client. At that I was not surprised. Everything became crystal clear, as if a ten-year fog were finally lifting. His fawning adoration by his female clients, the favors that so many did for him, financially and otherwise…and now he was probably afraid of the police.

Ruth, a client who'd started therapy with Chase over ten years ago, was also a member of his loyal therapy group. I recalled a group therapy/vacation at his place in Puerto Rico. A dozen of his regular clients and I were sunning ourselves on the warm sand. The water was calm, and Chase and Ruth were a distance away in the water. Were they bobbing up and down, floating with the waves, or were they having sex? Silly me.

No, stupid, stupid, stupid me. Immediately after I called him, he called the bank and transferred all the money in our office account into his own private account. Thousands of dollars for expenses, rent, and bills, plus *my* income, gone.

The only thing I didn't and couldn't know, until much later, was that psychopaths don't have partners, only victims.

One Cult Was Just Not Enough

I WANTED TO SPEAK WITH Dr. Virginia S. as soon as possible. Virginia was a sociology professor at Central Connecticut State College where Chase got his BSW and we both got our master's degrees. When he took courses with her, she introduced him to the beliefs and practices of her guru, Shri Kirpal Singh. I thought Chase had been initiated into that religion, and it was on that basis that Chase became my guru. In fact, early in my relationship with him, I traveled an hour out to her home in eastern Connecticut to attend a meditation with her and learn more about their guru and the Radhasoami tradition it was founded upon.

She was shocked when I told her about what happened to me, and then she told me about her *real* relationship with Chase. Yes, he was her student, and they did do hypnosis in her class. She told me, "He was an incredible hypnotist even then. I had him demonstrate trance induction in one of my classes. He managed to put the whole class under hypnosis. However, he was never an initiate of either Kirpal Singh or his successor, Darshan Singh. He was familiar with their teachings and only came for meditations a few times."

If Chase was not an initiate but the path was valid, as Virginia firmly believed, perhaps there was something here for me yet. I was very familiar with this tradition, as I believed I had been following it through Chase. Because of him, I had read all the literature about Kirpal Singh and the beliefs of the group.

107

I was grasping at straws. I desperately did not want to give everything up yet. To me, the alternative was the death of my spirituality and my beliefs about God. All or nothing.

I was initiated by Virginia's son Adam a few weeks later. In a ceremony not too different from the one I had when I started TM almost fifteen years ago, I was given my special mantra and began meditating. I guess if one doesn't learn from history, then history repeats itself.

Eager to be on the right spiritual path, I was excited to learn that Sant Darshan Singh was coming to the United States and holding a special retreat weekend. I signed up immediately.

The retreat was held in the quiet Connecticut countryside at what was, in the summer, a private camp. We stayed in bunks, then gathered at the meeting house dining room, with tables cleared to the side, for Darshan Singh's lectures and meditations.

We were told about how our souls would see certain lights as our souls developed. The first lights were blue, and I was so excited when I could see them in meditation! The next step was to rise above, into the clouds. Oh wow, I would now leave my body at last! Nooo. Not true. Didn't happen.

When the guru asked if anyone had any difficulty, I raised my hand, eager for his help. Coming over to my side, he pressed his thumb firmly over my "third eye" and asked me, "Now what do you see?" When I told him nothing happened, he grunted and walked away.

A light bulb finally came on in my head. *Bullshit.*

For the rest of the weekend, I watched him warily and noted his behavior and that of his followers. They looked just like Chase's group, with their awe and belief in all he said and did. But not I. Not now. Especially when I noticed one attractive woman gaining his attention and being given special audiences when others were turned away.

I was finally wising up. No more gurus. No more mystical, paranormal, spiritual anything. I was done. If God wasn't dead, he was not around anymore.

Exhausted, demoralized, angry, and depressed, I now had to face the results of my mindless search for meaning in life. There were so many victims of my beliefs and selfishness: my family first, then the clients who'd trusted me and looked to me for help. Could I ever fix the damage I had done to so many and repay the multilayered debts of pain? What did I do about my tremendous sense of shame and guilt?

I was ashamed of myself for allowing and abetting someone to hurt me, my family, and the innocent others who looked to me for help. I couldn't protect myself, let alone them. Would they forgive me? Could I ever forgive myself?

The feelings of guilt were overwhelming. Shame on me for allowing my beliefs in a magical and godlike (ha!) man to overshadow my own integrity. I remembered years ago reading a book on Tibetan mysticism, in which the guru commanded one of his followers to jump off a cliff. Just how far would I have gone if asked?

Mea culpa, mea culpa, mea maxima culpa.

Could I make amends? Could I repair myself enough to begin again? If so, how?

So what did I learn from that decade? I learned horrible, painful but important truths. It seems obvious now, but until that debacle, I believed that people were trustworthy, that they didn't intentionally lie or deceive. I also learned that not all who pose as friends are really friends. Not all who robe themselves in the garments of spirituality are holy.

Part 3

Freedom and Recovery

⟋⟍

WTF happened to me from 1977 to 1987? I had so many important questions.

1. What do I tell Ed and my family?
2. What do I tell my clients, and how do I help them, including those I inherited from Chase when he left?
3. What are the legal, ethical, and moral issues I need to deal with now?
4. Spirituality? What's that?
5. How can I heal from this?

Family First

POOR ED. AFTER I SPOKE with Kathy and Chase, I sat down with Ed. Though only peripherally involved these past few years in the aspects of my psychotherapy practice with Chase, he was nevertheless my partner in the whole undertaking.

Chase, he thought, was his friend too. Together, the four of us—Chase and Emma, Ed and I—had rebuilt several houses, vacationed together, and ridden our ATVs up and down the Connecticut River. Ed was my backup, my rock. Throughout our marriage, he was regarded as Saint Ed by my family and me for putting up with all my idiocies and crazy choices.

I finally gathered the courage to talk with him. To level with him as best I could about the reality of those years. No more secrets. I shared my beliefs about who I'd thought Chase was and how I thought that I and the family would benefit from knowing and being with him. Ed listened carefully and said little. As I shared with him what had been happening to this point, I could feel and see the hurt on his face. He was very hurt. Silent but angry.

I had trusted Chase, and Ed had trusted me. I was betrayed by that trust, and in turn, I had betrayed Ed's. I apologized, but how do you adequately apologize for ten years of pain and lies? For thousands of dollars in savings gone up in smoke? How could I possibly make up or atone for the damage that I had done to our relationship?

I wanted—no, I *needed*—to make amends to him and the kids as well. Alli was now seventeen and Jason sixteen. I sat the children down separately and from the bottom of my heart told them how sorry I was to have brought this man into our lives. I asked them to forgive me, and they did. But how could I fully explain to them what had happened to me, to us, if I didn't understand myself? I was and am extremely grateful for their patience, love, and kindness as we all grappled with the ramifications of having had what I now know was a sociopath in our midst.

I found a lawyer in a further attempt at closure, and I sued Chase for the money he'd stolen from us over the years in our real estate dealings and from our office account. We won a few thousand dollars, a fraction of what we'd lost, but we had a huge gain in satisfaction.

At a break during the legal deposition in Chase's lawyer's office, I ran into him on the way to the bathroom. He was being deposed by my lawyers at the same time. For the first time in over a year, we met face to face. I stared him down hard, without speaking. He in turn avoided eye contact, changed direction, and slunk away quickly. I knew he was afraid of me. Coward. He'd once told me he wished I was a man and could accompany him on his adventures. For what, protection?

Ed with Yogi Bear

What a pathetic excuse of a human being he was. From rage to pity to forgiveness. All in stages, with the last one taking years. I found that holding onto my anger was too self-destructive. Chase never felt nor cared about anyone else's feelings. To hold onto the anger was a waste of energy and stopped me from moving past the pain of those years. Forgiveness meant letting go of the attachment I had to caring about him or hoping for revenge. I let him go to whatever hell or heaven he deserved. I let God deal with him. In any case, that was when I got my third English mastiff, Yogi Bear, who weighed 213 pounds!

As far as I know, Cathy and the girls were too frightened of him to go to the police. Chase retreated to safety in Florida and I resumed taking Kung fu and mixed martial arts classes.

Our Clients Are Victims Too

⌒

WHAT SHOULD I DO NOW with my clients? I had inherited Chase's group and others who were in individual therapy with him. I sought supervision and found a psychologist at the Institute of Living, a respected private psychiatric hospital in Hartford, who helped me sort out the complex issues that faced me. He suggested, "You need to terminate all of Chase's clients and refer them to other therapists." He gave me a list of those he knew and trusted. Then he said, "You also need to go into therapy yourself and get some help in dealing with this."

No kidding! I strongly agreed to both suggestions.

With much trepidation, I entered the group room at my office that Wednesday evening. I had gone over and over what I was going to say to them, and nothing felt good. Would they be angry with Chase, with me? Would they want the thousands of dollars they'd spent in that office for therapy(?) returned? Would they sue?

I met with all fifteen and told them what I had learned about Chase. They deserved the truth. Gently, I told them that he had left to live with Ruth, a former group member, in Florida. Some already knew about this, having heard it from her. For others, this was a shock.

With much anxiety, I decided to tell them about the abuse of Cathy's children. Some of them were parents themselves, and they needed to be aware of any contact he might have had with their kids.

The betrayal of trust in this person whom they had held up on a pedestal was devastating.

"Each time I see a red Jeep, I think he is spying on me!" one long-term client revealed to me. To my surprise, she wasn't the only one afraid of him. Why? What had he said or done to them over those years that produced fear? What threats had he made? Of disclosure, of poor treatment, of sexual abuse? Then I remembered the multiple times he'd led the group in guided meditations. What instructions/commands/warnings had he given them—and me?

I told them about the supervision I had turned to, to help me help them. I told them that my supervisor strongly suggested that they find another therapist who could help them work through some of these very complex issues. I told them that I agreed with him that this was the best path for them for their healing and that I had a list of recommended therapists from him that would help them move forward.

Upon hearing this, their first reaction was silence, then fear. They still believed Chase to be very powerful and were afraid he would be angry with them. They believed me when I shared with them what I knew. Those who were angry at him became, understandably, angry with me. I felt powerless to help them.

To my surprise, only two left. Others, I suspect, were afraid to leave. I was the only other therapist they knew, and I was very familiar with both their clinical issues and the "treatment" they had had. After several years they were also close friends with each other.

After Chase left, I needed to leave the office we had shared. Too many bad memories. I spoke with the building owner and got another office on another floor that had a different layout. Slowly, over time, the rest of his old clients terminated counseling with me.

It took another a year to finally move out of that building in Hartford and find another office nearby in East Hartford. It was a new building, with a totally different feel and look. I needed to make a clean break. I found another therapist to work with me and share expenses. We both had new clients who had never met or heard of Chase.

The Long Road
to Recovery

I BEGAN THERAPY TOO. THAT produced new problems. After I described my ten-year ordeal, one therapist after another tried to suggest or explain my experience as the aftermath of sexual abuse in childhood. "If you think you were abused, you probably were," according to the popular self-help books of the time.

Gullible idiot that I was, I even began to believe it myself, questioning my brother and sister about memories none of us had. Thankfully my father had died several years before and was spared the anguish of accusation. I kept silent about this to my mother, fearful of how this would likely push her over the edge. Like her sister, she too had a major depressive episode after the death of her husband. I wasn't depressed; I was angry, temporarily displacing my anger at Chase onto my father and back again.

The first therapist, referred by a friend, was Dr. R. Based on my description of Chase and my denial of his sexual abuse of his clients, she believed *I* must have been abused by him too, and before that by my father! How else could I have gotten into such a relationship?

Dr. R practiced a type of therapy called transactional analysis, which was popular in the '70s and '80s. In TA, put very simply, a parent teaches a child, the child feels the concepts taught by its parent, and the adult learns it and carries it on in behavior. To fix this, the patient analyzes the stuck behavior, thoughts, and feelings and then hopefully redefines them. Then, to treat my bottomless pit of anger, now displaced upon my father, Dr. R gave me a stick and had me beat a pillow.

"There, get that anger out!" So there I was, with a group of other "abused" women, yelling at and beating pillows. Of course, that didn't help, so I sought another therapist.

I made an appointment with Dr. M, a highly regarded psychiatrist, for hypnosis and treatment. That did not help either. I did not recall any episodes of assault by my father, thank God. Sorry, Dad!

Dr. M was a poor choice of a doctor. In addition to supporting the idea of abuse, he told me that my episode of bliss in meditation was simply an endorphin dump, "a bowel movement of the brain." Another blow to any thoughts of spiritual growth. I left him after that, totally disillusioned.

The third doc I tried agreed to see me for a consult at no charge. That was refreshing all by itself. After listening to my story, now well rehearsed, he folded his and my fingers into a temple, looked me in the eye, and said, "You are now safe, and all will be well. You are in good hands with me." I left that office quickly at the end of the session and did not make another appointment. He truly scared me. Another Chase?

This was in the mid-80's, when memories of childhood sexual abuse were suddenly being remembered by adults for the first time in therapy facilitated by many mental health professionals. If a therapist believes that hidden memories are the cause of a client's problems, then through direct or indirect suggestion, seeds of suspicion can be planted, which then grow like weeds. Once a person accepts that they were abused in childhood, it is extremely difficult for them to later disbelieve it.

False memory syndrome (FMS) activists, mostly parents, whom I previously dismissed as misguided and mistaken, were gaining prominence. They accused therapists of installing, instigating, and promoting memories of sexual abuse, including Satanic ritual abuse, often when there wasn't any. Parents were now suing the therapists, and adult children were suing their parents.

To their credit, the FMS activists fought against the tendency by some mental health clinicians to blame any problems their patients have on parental sexual abuse. Though statistically there was no proof to support their contention that sudden memories recalled in therapy were false, through litigation, they did put a caution brake on mental health clinicians that was long overdue. It also spurred some excellent research into how the mind remembers and forgets, and also how it misremembers.

Cult? What's That?

I DON'T RECALL WHEN I began wondering if what I was in was a cult. The Unification Church was making news at that time, due to its mass weddings of thousands of people who were strangers to each other. Reverend Moon was its adored leader and received much publicity. Another cult in Oregon led by an Indian guru was accused of poisoning a town outside their ashram. I asked myself how people could be so blindly accepting of someone! Duh...

I looked up the definition of a cult. An article on cultism in the *Cultic Studies Journal* explained it this way: "Cult (totalist type): A group or movement exhibiting a great or excessive devotion or dedication to some person, idea, or thing and employing unethically manipulative techniques of persuasion and control (e.g., isolation from former friends and family, debilitation, use of special methods to heighten suggestibility and subservience, powerful group pressures, information management, suspension of individuality or critical judgment, promotion of total dependency on the group and fear of leaving it), designed to advance the goals of the group's leaders, to the actual or possible detriment of members, their families, or the community."

Much of that fit my relationship with Chase.

Perhaps it was an announcement of a meeting in a nearby town of the Cult Awareness Network. I had never heard about it before. At that time, CAN was an organization of mostly parents who met for support and information about how to deal with their adult children who were in destructive cults.

The local chapter had about thirty members present that evening. All of them were parents and family of cult members There were no cult or former cult members at the meeting. They looked at me very oddly when I introduced myself. Venturing out to listen to what they said was eye opening.

I wanted to know if what I was involved with was really a cult. That meant finding a therapist who specialized in this field. That was not easy. There was literally no one in Connecticut knowledgeable at that time about cults. The closest was Lorna Goldberg, a clinical social worker and a serious researcher of anything related to cults and mind control. She was highly regarded by those in CAN, so I made an appointment and traveled the two hours down to New Jersey from Connecticut to see her.

We first explored my vulnerabilities at the time of meeting Chase. I was a mother of two young children who was working full time, as well as going to college. I was deeply involved in mysticism and had already been initiated into one cult, Transcendental Meditation. Through meditation and my interest in spirituality, I was attracted to those who could answer my questions about the meaning of life and pathways to God. Both Father Ted and Chase fit the bill. But Ted's interest and friendship was one of parity. In no way did he take advantage of my interests and naivete.

It was very different with Chase. His spirituality, as he taught it, was based on Eastern mysticism. Because of his hypnosis and suggestion, I believed that he was indeed a wise person who could guide both my professional and spiritual development. When I joined his psychotherapy practice and invested money in this "partnership," I gave him some control over my financial resources, which increased in our real estate endeavors. Time, money, effort, and spiritual goals. It started out looking so hopeful, so promising. She validated that what I described had all the hallmarks of a cult: deception, dependency, and dread.

After our initial interview, I stayed for Lorna's support group for ex-members of cults. I heard their stories, problems, and issues after leaving their groups—all kinds of groups! I was amazed to hear about New Age, Eastern, Christian, and even Jewish cults.

A Healing Regression
for Understanding

NOW THAT I COULD BEGIN to comprehend what had happened to me, I could begin to recover. I asked Lorna for a referral to a reputable hypnotherapist to uncover what was done to me during that "weight loss" session with Chase, which I believed was the beginning of my entrapment. I didn't know that it really began at that first lunch with him and Georgia.

Lorna referred me to a psychologist in Rochester, New York, a six-hour drive from home in Connecticut. Since my daughter was also attending college in Rochester, it turned out to be convenient. I kept that appointment with the doctor, fearful of what I would uncover but mostly curious about what I would learn.

"I have no memory at all of that hypnosis for weight loss," I explained, after giving the psychologist some history of my relationship with Chase. "I need to know as well if there were any remaining suggestions I might have that were keeping me under his influence or are affecting my behavior in any way now."

"I can't make any promises, but we will see what comes up," he replied cautiously.

If Lorna hadn't vouched for him, I would never have allowed anyone to hypnotize me again. Ed waited patiently in the waiting room, as he was supportive of my healing.

I went into trance easily and deeply. We then reviewed the suggestions that Chase had given me while I was in trance, some of which were:

> *You will lose weight as long as you listen to me. Just look at me*
> *when you have questions, and you will know the answers.*
>
> *I am wise and enlightened. It is your karma that brought*
> *you to me. I am the most important person you will ever know.*
>
> *Through me, and only through me, all your spiritual*
> *and material needs and desires will be met, but only if you are*
> *obedient.*
>
> *I will always know everything that you think and feel. There*
> *is nothing you can hide from me.*
>
> *Each time you see or think of me, these suggestions will get*
> *stronger.*
>
> *You will obey me always or else you will die spiritually.*

And then I remembered that he'd touched my breast, at which I came
out of trance abruptly.

I left that office in a state of shock but relieved to know the truth.
It answered so many questions. And it was all bullshit. The suggestions
were dispelled once I understood them, and they no longer had any
power over me anymore. I was so happy to see Ed, waiting patiently for
me with a big hug. I shared with him what I learned. Everything but the
last part.

I have heard it repeatedly said by those who practice hypnotherapy,
from a variety of different training programs, that you cannot force
someone to behave against their will. I no longer believe that. The subject enters treatment to make a change. That is entirely voluntary. They
are reassured that their control of themselves will not be changed or
altered, nor will they be made to do something that they would otherwise not choose. No Manchurian candidates here. However, a clever and
manipulative operator can make his or her hypnotic suggestions seem
appropriate, important, or beneficial to the client by making subtle suggestions *over time* that can overcome normal resistance. The distinction

here is over time, and the small, incremental behavioral changes then become the new normal. Another big difference is that through suggestion, the client may have *no* recall of the discussion and the commands made while in trance.

Then I found Dr. Betty R. She was a psychologist who did not practice hypnosis but rather cognitive behavioral therapy. She explored with me the meaning of my experiences, the thoughts, feelings, and beliefs about that time, and how they affected my choices and behavior. I now understood and accepted that I had been in a psychotherapy cult. I understood how I got there and how to heal from it.

The Cult Awareness
Network

I WENT TO MY FIRST national Cult Awareness Network meeting in 1988. I didn't know what to expect other than that Lorna would be a speaker, along with other nationally known experts in the fields of mental health, law, and sociology. Over three hundred people were in attendance, divided among parents and family of cult members, mental health workers and researchers, and former members of cults. There were lectures and support sessions for each that I could attend.

While there, I will never forget entering a meeting room for ex-members only. I quietly sat in the rear of the room and listened as many of the forty or fifty people shared their stories of their time in their cults. I was shocked at the number and variety of destructive groups and the profound damage wrought by them. There were religious cults, including Eastern (Hindu and Buddhist), Western (Christian, Jewish, and Muslim), and New Age; UFO cults such as Heaven's Gate; martial arts cults; and of course psychotherapy cults. All were defined and led by an endless variety of charismatic leaders who used a variety of manipulative techniques to control and take advantage of members.

At the break, I joined other women crying in the restrooms. I was not alone anymore. I discovered friends and peers who were also former cult members, as well as those in the mental health field, that I would treasure for the rest of my life.

I also learned that after the cult, many:

1. Join a "safe" religion, such as a mainstream church.
2. Join another cult.
3. Have no religion at all and are spiritually dead.

I did/was all three.

It was natural for me to become an activist. I joined CAN and became president of the Connecticut chapter. I also joined the International Cultic Studies Association (ICSA), a leading research and educational group dedicated to helping mental health professionals, families, and former members of cults, as well as the legal profession, to understand and heal from cultic involvement.

In trying to understand how these cult leaders were so able to entrap thousands of people, I began researching the psychopathology of socio-paths and psychopaths, starting with the works of Herve Cleckley and Robert Hare.

Was Chase a Psychopath?

A YEAR AFTER I JOINED CAN, I gave my first talk at the annual conference in Seattle on the psychopathology of cult leaders. Talking about this was very therapeutic, and I actually felt like I was taking revenge against Chase and all the other monsters leading cults. It later became a chapter in my first book, *Captive Hearts/Captive Minds*, and it has remained my favorite talk and most healing chapter.

I was able to see each of these characteristics in Chase and all the other cult leaders I heard and read about. Dr. Robert Hare describes the characteristics of psychopaths in his book *Without Conscience: The Disturbing World of the Psychopaths Among Us*. I have added some examples of his behavior here:

1. *Glibness/superficial charm.* They exude self-confidence, they are persuasive, entertaining and charming. Chase drew people to him with his smile and easy laugh. You were either strongly drawn to him or repulsed.
2. *Manipulative and conning.* They do not recognize the rights of others. As a social worker, I assumed he was looking out for others' welfare. Wrong! There were no checks on his behavior. Psychopaths often make an ally out of their future victims, then dispose of them. That's me!
3. *Grandiose sense of self.* Always the center of attention, everything is owed to them as their right, and they have an insatiable need for

adulation. I observed that immediately when my Porsche bested his Datson. He couldn't/wouldn't take second place in anything. Later, he needed a phony doctorate to be superior to me and my advanced nursing degrees.

4. *Pathological lying.* It is almost impossible for them to be consistently truthful about either a major or minor issue. The only "truth" is what will best meet their needs. Psychopaths are extremely convincing and forceful in the expression of their views and often pass lie detector tests. As a person who values integrity, I was not prepared for the opposite. I was quite naïve!

5. *Lack of remorse, shame, or guilt.* They see others around them as objects, targets, or opportunities, not as people. Master manipulators, psychopaths and malignant narcissists (a close relative) do not have friends; they have victims and accomplices, with the accomplices frequently ending up as victims. The ends always justify the means.

6. *Shallow emotions.* While they may have outbursts of emotion, more often than not, they are putting on a calculated response to obtain certain results. Positive feelings of warmth, joy, love, and compassion are more often feigned than experienced. It was not possible to read Chase's emotions as he was a great actor and con artist.

7. *Incapacity for love.* I could recall a time early in our relationship when I told him how much he was loved by his clients and friends. "Nobody loves me", was his blunt and honest response. This was a rare and brief moment when the mask came off.

8. *Need for stimulation.* Chase lived on the edge. Motorcycles, fast cars and multiple sexual partners which only came to light after he left.

9. *Callousness/lack of empathy.* Chase used his people skills to exploit, abuse, and wield power, especially over his clients. I mistook his silence as caring, but he was truly unable to empathize with the pain of his victims. Only his pain was real to him. Then others paid the price. Even pets were not immune, as I caught him badly

teasing his father's cat. This was the only time in 10 years that my reaction was enough to stop his behavior. I can only suspect he did worse with his dog.

10. *Poor behavioral controls/impulsive behavior.* I didn't see this until much later in our relationship and learned about it mostly from Cathy. After he left, I was surprised by how some of his former clients were frightened of him. What did he tell them when they were in altered (hypnotic) states?

11. *Early behavior problems/juvenile delinquency.* Cult leaders frequently have a history of behavioral and academic difficulties. Fred, Chase's childhood friend, revealed his criminal past to me and his choice to go into the military or go to jail. Fred briefly joined the mortgage company, but for unknown (to me) reasons didn't stay long. I didn't realize how much difficulty Chase had during our master's degree program using clients to do his homework and write his papers!

12. *Irresponsibility/unreliability.* Not concerned about the consequences of their behavior, they leave behind the wreckage of other people's lives and dreams. Chase never accepted blame for any failures or mistakes. He was totally indifferent to the damage he did to others. It was always someone else's fault. Mine of course!

13. *Promiscuous sexual behavior/infidelity.* Marital fidelity is rare in their life. Previously noted!

14. *Lack of realistic life plan/parasitic lifestyle.* Leaders of cults tend to move around a lot, making countless efforts at starting new business or seeking new and fertile ground to exploit. Chase moved around a lot, using others' talents and abilities to start new businesses in Connecticut as well as in Puerto Rico, such as in real estate and the mortgage company.

Exit Counseling vs. Deprogramming

THERE ARE MANY WAYS TO leave a cult. With some, the leader dies, and no other extreme narcissist comes forth to take over the group. In my case, the leader chose to leave, possibly to avoid the police or a lawsuit. In other cases, severe disillusionment may cause a drifting away, and some leave when the family decides to engage in exit counseling. This is an intervention similar to one done with someone who has a drug or alcohol abuse problem. These are planned meetings between the family and a team of professionals who use an educational model to have the member reach an informed decision about whether to stay in or leave the group.

Interventions, a.k.a. exit counseling, are voluntary. Typically, the family invites their loved one to visit, and when the family members enter and explain their presence, the cult member can refuse to take part or can leave at any time. This is not a "deprogramming," which was an earlier and extreme attempt at getting members out of cults by "snatching and confining" the person. In the half-dozen interventions I took part in, we never kidnapped anyone. They were *all* voluntary.

As a mental health worker, I was invited by a few of those teams on their interventions when the mental health of a family member was an issue. On each case I was involved in, I gained a deeper appreciation of the entanglement of the issues between family and cult, and between the cult and the individual.

I was invited on my first intervention by the late Kevin Garvey. I had met Kevin at a CAN meeting. He lived in Connecticut too, and we got to know each other. I was very impressed with his keen intellect and vast knowledge of the different groups.

The family had contacted him about exit counseling their daughter out of a New Age cult. He provided initial information about the process, and when they professed concern about their daughter's emotional fragility, he asked me if I would join him and Joe Kelly on the intervention.

"Absolutely! I would love to be included!" I responded immediately. I was intrigued and excited and wanted to help. I had met Joe and his partner, Pat Ryan, at my first CAN meeting the previous year. Both former members of TM, we related to each other instantly and became dear friends.

Mr. and Mrs. T lived in a modest suburban home north of New Haven. They shared their anxiety and concerns about their daughter Jeannie's increasing alienation from the family. I listened as they described her defensiveness about the group as well as her requests for money to take their programs and attend lectures. Her contact with the family became less and less frequent, and they were afraid they were going to lose her completely to the group. They also described her as "emotionally fragile" since adolescence and told me they were relieved I had agreed to be a part of the intervention.

Kevin and Joe had already met with the family, interviewing them extensively and explaining what was involved in an intervention. They planned how to invite their daughter to the home, and what they would say and do to invite her to stay and listen to us. That was the critical part! Kevin made it very clear that Jeannie would know that listening to what we had to say about mind control and cults was completely voluntary, and she could leave any time she wished.

When a date was set for the intervention, we booked our rooms at the Holiday Inn and spent the night drinking coffee and precisely planning the next few days. We reviewed the information we'd received from the family and then discussed what information could/would be helpful. I learned that with Kevin, a reformed alcoholic, every night would involve staying up late drinking coffee and planning. But he was brilliant, and I learned much from him.

The intervention went well and smoothly, much to my relief. When we got to the family's home, Jeannie was already there. She did not know we were coming. When her parents let us in, she looked up, surprised and alarmed.

"We invited them here because we love you and are concerned about your involvement with the group. We hope you will stay and listen to them. If you wish to leave, you can, but we love you and hope you stay," her parents pleaded.

Kevin quickly took over and reassured her about our presence. "It's important for you to know that you can leave any time you wish. No one will make you stay."

It worked. Her initial guard slowly came down. We showed her a film, *Captive Minds*, which is a classic on how hypnosis works. In the film, a teacher in a college classroom demonstrates a trance induction, making some suggestions to a student volunteer, which the student unknowingly follows. The class is amazed, and the student is incredulous when he is brought out of trance.

We spent the next two days exploring what mind-control techniques her group used, her beliefs about the leader, and the efficacy of his teachings.

"How did you know this? Where did you get this information? What proof did you have about..." Jeannie did beautifully! She asked many questions, first defensively, then with interest. Once she understood more about the deception that was used against her, she was able to question the teachings, and her own doubts about the group surfaced. That's when we all took a sigh of relief. Our job was done. We referred Jeannie and her family to support groups in the area.

I also became aware of the dangers involved when those who do the interventions are helping families whose member belongs to dangerous as well as destructive group. Being sued, followed, and having property destroyed were hidden dangers I learned about. Some of my exit counseling friends were harassed, threatened, and sued by the cults if the interventions failed. I was lucky. The closest I came to being confronted by a cult myself was when I was deposed in a lawsuit against a prominent international cult. I was counseling an ex-member of a notorious cult. When she felt well enough, she hired a lawyer and sued them to recover the several thousands of dollars for courses she took, and the damages that resulted from them. As her therapist, I was subpoenaed to testify in a deposition.

"Why do you think the group is using mind control? How do you define a cult? Why is this or that not true? How do you know?" These and hundreds of other questions were hammered at me.

Remembering my hypnosis training in neuro-linguistic programming, I turned the tables on these two very aggressive lawyers that morning. Speaking slowly and evenly, maintaining eye contact, and using the same language with a different tone, I answered, "A cult is…Your group does this…" I went on for the next three hours. As a result, their speech slowed, their belligerence lessened and their questioning stopped.

Then we had a lunch break. They must have consulted with their group in the meantime, because they came back with a vengeance and hammered me for the next three hours. But the group lost their case, and my client was able to collect an unannounced sum for damages.

Don't Call Me Doctor

FINALLY, AFTER TEN YEARS OF being known as Madeleine Tobias, PsyD, I realized it was time to give it up. I was falsely representing my credentials. I had now been involved with the ICSA for a couple of years, and I was living a lie with the people I knew and cared about. Many were now dear friends who gave me support, respect, and love.

I decided that at the next annual ICSA conference, I would drop the "Dr. Tobias." Anxious, I stood on the stage, at the podium, took a breath, and began to speak to the four hundred people gathered before me. I didn't know how they would react and was afraid it would destroy our relationships when I revealed my deception.

"You all know the topic of my talk today is *'Don't Call Me Doctor.'* Well, I really mean it. I have a confession to make." I took a deep breath and then went on to explain, "I got my doctorate in psychology while in my cult. My leader suggested that we both get this degree from Heed University, so we did. We both wrote our dissertations, and we each paid the $3,000 for tuition, and that was all I needed to do.

I can no longer live this lie, especially to all of you, whom I respect and care about. I hope you will forgive me. I hope for your understanding and acceptance."

I shared my feelings then about being an obedient member of what was a psychotherapy cult, and my feelings now of being out and burdened by an untruth, a lie. I needed to give it up openly.

I didn't know what reaction I would get. Sitting before me in the audience were mental health professionals, former members of various cults and their families, plus a few lawyers. To my great relief, I first saw their surprise, and then, when I was finished, they gave me standing applause. Many hugs, handshakes, and even a few kisses. What a relief!

The Dark Side

⌒

WHILE IN PRIVATE PRACTICE IN East Hartford, I got a strange referral from Father Malachi Martin. Malachi was a Jesuit priest and a well-known Church exorcist. Kevin had insisted I talk with Father Martin. I called him, and we talked for a several minutes on the phone as I explained who I was and my work with Kevin.

He then urged me to let him know the next time I was in the New York City, and he invited me to dinner. Not long afterward, I met him in Manhattan at his elegant brownstone apartment, and we went out to eat at a fine French restaurant. Malachi was charming. I had read his book, *Hostage to the Devil*, which I later learned was the basis for the movie *The Exorcist*. We talked about a wide range of subjects, from cults and religion to deeply personal spiritual issues I was having with the Church.

About a year later, when Malachi called, he took me by surprise. I was sitting in my office in East Hartford, in between appointments.

"Can you see a family for me?" he asked. "I would like you to evaluate the son. He's about eleven years old."

"Malachi, I don't see kids. I just work with adults." I thanked him for thinking of me but told him that I had no expertise working with children. Besides, the family lived in NYC, and surely there was someone, if not a multitude of therapists, in New York who could help.

"But I want *you* to see him," he calmly insisted. So, curious, I agreed. I made an appointment with the family, and the following week, the mother drove up to Connecticut with her son, Matthew.

Neatly dressed, Matthew looked like any other preadolescent boy. The history I got from his mother was that Matthew and his brother were adopted as toddlers, and his childhood prior to recent events had apparently been normal. However, a few weeks ago, he had collected flammable materials and gasoline, hiding them in the basement.

"He set fire to the house while we were all sleeping! Thank God one of us awoke, and we were all able to escape. The house was completely destroyed!"

I sat with Matthew alone and asked him to tell me about this in his own words. Without any hesitation, he calmly looked at me and related, in a matter-of-fact voice, "I bought the gasoline and hid it in the basement until I was ready. I couldn't wait for them to go to bed. I waited some more until I was pretty sure they were all asleep. I had disconnected all the fire alarms in the house, but Dad was a light sleeper. He must have heard or smelled the fire. It was loud and stunk. I just wanted to watch and see them die." He said with a shrug and a smirk.

Throughout, he stared intently at my face to watch my reaction. As he talked, I saw the irises of his green eyes turn into horizontal slits, like a goat's. I felt as if I was in the presence of pure evil. My body went cold, and a chill spread down my back. I tried not to visibly react to his performance. He scared the shit out of me. I couldn't wait to get them out of my office!

When he finished talking, I quickly ended the session and sent him and his mother back to NYC with the assurance I would call Father Martin. Which I did.

"Malachi, I watched his eyes!" I told him briefly what I heard and observed. He listened quietly, thanked me, and said no more. Of this I am certain: Malachi knew exactly what was happening with that child, but he wanted me to know it too. He was familiar with evil, and he wanted me to know it really exists.

No End of Learning

IN MY LAST YEARS IN Connecticut, I realized there is no end to learning and growth.

"You must see my father!" a client of mine pleaded. "He is horribly depressed, and I don't know how to help him. I don't even know if I can get him to come here."

"Okay, just let me know, and I will make time for him," I agreed.

Not too long afterward, he came to my office, a teary-eyed, middle-aged man who appeared much older than his forty-five years. Hesitating, he picked the least comfortable chair in my office to sit in. Perched on its edge, he fidgeted as I encouraged him to tell me why he came.

"My daughter wouldn't stop bugging me. I shouldn't be here. I don't think you or anyone can help me. I don't deserve anything!" he said angrily. He then proceeded to tell me what had happened two years ago.

"I was just driving down the street. I don't even know if I was going too fast. I wasn't drinking." And then he hesitated before spilling it out, crying. "She just ran in front of me chasing a ball, and I couldn't stop! I hit and killed her! It's all my fault. I should've gone slower; I should've seen her!"

He was right. I didn't know how to help him. I listened calmly and offered support, which he refused. He denied being suicidal, but I did not believe him. I was glad his daughter was being watchful.

This was before my training in Eye Movement Desensitization and Reprocessing (EMDR), and I didn't have a clue how to help him with that horrific trauma. He did not want another appointment, and he never returned. I do not know what happened to him, and I hoped and prayed he got the help he needed.

I knew I needed to know more. His pain and my failure to help him became the impetus for me to continue learning and growing as a therapist.

EMDR sounded hopeful for the treatment of trauma. I soon began training and using it with some success. More about it in the next chapter.

Forgiveness

WHAT HAS HAUNTED ME FOR years is how to pay back all that I took from others during my time in the cult. With my family, it has been simple: being the best wife and mother I could be to Ed and the kids. It has been more difficult with those who were harmed emotionally and financially in the ten years with Chase, whom I would never encounter again.

My role with my former clients was over. I did the best I could to help them come to terms with those years with Chase. Learning to forgive *myself* for enabling him was an important lesson.

Forgiving him was easier than forgiving myself.

I began by continuing to offer my counseling services on a sliding scale, and occasionally at no cost, to those who had been in cults. I held a free monthly support group for former members in my office, and I traveled throughout the United States and Canada, speaking without compensation at Cult Awareness Network and the International Cultic Studies Association conferences on mental health issues. I contributed chapters to books that raised money for the ICSA. The first one was *Recovery From Cults* (1993), and then *Cult Recovery: A Clinician's Guide* (2017). That all felt good. It felt good to give back to those who'd helped me and to pay it forward to others. That has not stopped.

Until CAN was sued out of existence by Scientology, I was the president of the Connecticut chapter and was available to families and ex-members for support. I made an appearance on *The Sally Jessy Raphael*

Show, then later on *The Oprah Winfrey Show,* to help educate the public about the dangers of destructive cults.

Will it ever be enough? When does it stop being payback and start being loving and altruistic service to others? Perhaps just asking the question is its own answer.

In 1993, Ed's manufacturing job was transferred to New Hampshire. I was relieved and happy. I closed my private practice, said goodbye to some wonderful friends and left all traces of Dr. Charles Sanborn and Associates behind. I Googled his name annually until finally, in 2008, I found his death notice. No further information was available or needed. I was very ready for my new life up north.

> The day the child realizes that all adults are imperfect,
> He becomes an adolescent;
> The day he forgives them, he becomes an adult;
> The day he forgives himself, he becomes wise.
> —Alden Nowlan

Part 4

Way Up North to Vermont

New Hampshire and Catholic Again?

IT TOOK JUST ONE DAY to pack up the furniture in the house but another three days for the movers to pack up all the stuff just in the basement. Ed had saved *everything* since we got married twenty-six years earlier—tools, books, old furniture, paperwork, you name it. Thank God his company picked up all the moving expenses and bought the house when it didn't sell. It was now 1993, and Connecticut was going through its own recession. People were putting bumper stickers on their cars that read, "Will the last one to leave Connecticut please turn off the lights?"

After we found a lovely home in New Hampshire and moved in, I had nothing to do. My psychotherapy practice, volunteer work with the International Cultic Studies Association, friends—all gone. Finished, done. There were only so many books, mostly detective novels, I could read. I had worked full or part time since I graduated nursing school thirty years ago. Now nothing. I knew no one.

We lived fifteen hundred feet up a mountain—okay, a big hill—on a rural road, with no close neighbors but a great view of Mount Ascutney in Vermont. Our house looked down upon the nearby town of Plainfield, but we could not see it below the morning clouds that rolled in from the nearby Connecticut River.

At least Ed met lots of coworkers in his new job who soon became friends. I stayed in my PJs or sweats for much of the day, unless I went food shopping. I was going crazy from boredom.

I learned that people from northern New England—Maine, New Hampshire, and Vermont—notoriously avoided those who moved up there. We were looked down upon as flatlanders. In turn, we called them woodchucks. If you didn't have three generations in the graveyard, you were a newcomer. They were *not* friendly. They just stared at me when I passed by. Not even a wave or smile.

And I wanted a horse. Here we were, living in a rural community in New Hampshire, with lots of opportunity for riding. Too bad that buying and keeping horses were so horribly expensive. My book *Captive Hearts/ Captive Minds* had just been published, and the expected income from consultations and exit counseling did not appear, despite my appearance on *Oprah Winfrey*. Appearing on *Oprah*, though—now that was fun! Not only did I receive an invitation to the show, but they paid for my flight, all meals, and a room in a fancy hotel. I even discovered my favorite dessert—crème brûlée, which was served at the hotel both at dinner and breakfast. There were former cult members on the show, and Oprah held up my book for the cameras! I got to say a few words, and it was over. I still have my Thanks, Oprah! mug.

I appeared on the show, but the show did not appear on TV. On the scheduled day, O. J. Simpson did his highly aired Bronco ride through southern Los Angeles, preempting everything on the air worldwide. Domino's Pizza reported record sales, probably because people were glued to their TV sets.

Months later, my old friend Alex called me, laughing. "Mady, your voice woke me up at three a.m.! You and Oprah talking. I guess I left the TV on when I went to bed."

"Alex, that show was taped months ago. It never aired until last night?"

So much for bad karma. No fame, no money, no horse. I think this was the first book shown on *Oprah* that did not become a best seller!

Thankfully another engineer and his wife had been transferred with Ed. I got to know Karen, and we became friends. She too was ignored by everyone she met here. We banded together, looking for something to do. Because they were Catholic, I attended church with her, and I again became a Catholic. This time it stuck, at least for a while. I liked the priest.

I became involved in RCIA, the Rite of Christian Initiation of Adults, and learned more about the Church, the rituals, and the sacraments. Not someone to do anything halfway, I also became a lector at Mass and eventually a eucharistic minister. I enjoyed it immensely and found it fulfilling to be a Catholic for the first time, active in *my* church.

Administering the Eucharist brought me into that special realm of altered consciousness I had not experienced in many years. I was also able to separate the spirituality of the sacraments from the history of the Church.

Then I took a tour organized by the archdiocese to the holy sites of Fatima and Lourdes. Any excuse to travel! It became one of the highlights of my time in the Church. I traveled both as a Jew trying to put aside my harsh judgments of the Church and as an objective observer of the other pilgrims' religiosity. I didn't witness any miracles, but I loved the journey through Spain, Portugal, and France by bus with thirty others, accompanied by two priests from the archdiocese. I was awed by the ancient cities of Barcelona, Lisbon, and the towns and countryside of France, which were hundreds of years older than my world here in the States. Their cobblestone streets, upscale restaurants, and sophisticated shopping and residents made me self-conscious of my fanny pack, jeans and sneakers.

I loved being a tourist, but I was not a pilgrim. I was curiously un-moved spiritually by the sites so holy to Catholics.

I looked at and wandered through the huge cathedrals. I was awed by their beauty, artwork, and architecture, but they were only history for me, though of deep spiritual significance for my fellow travelers. They kept reminding me of my Jewishness, and worse, the Inquisition, which coexisted with and was caused by these same religious institutions. Death and holiness. Convert or die.

But I still have the small bottle of holy water from Lourdes.

At the end of the trip, while waiting for the plane in the airport to take us home, one of our group members started to hallucinate and became delusional, believing herself to be a holy saint. As she rambled on about who she was and what was (not) happening around her, I be-came very alarmed for her safety. She was clearly psychotic and was not in touch with who or where she was. She was unable to interact with me when I tried to talk with her and ground her.

Then I pleaded with our two priests, who were ensconced at the air-port lounge with their drinks. "We need help! Sarah has gone off the deep end. She is hallucinating and thinks she is in Jerusalem. Please come quickly!"

"She'll be okay. Just leave her alone," replied the priests, who were taking a break from us. When I told them about my fears for her, they just looked at me, tired and uninterested. Nothing! They didn't even get up from their chairs.

Uh oh. Another shelf was being built in the closet of my mind, this one labeled "Catholic stuff." Then I shut the closet door. I and the other group members watched over Sarah as we made it safely back to the States and returned her to her family.

What became of her I don't know. I found out later that this was not an unusual occurrence for some who travel to Israel and other holy sites. They call it the Jerusalem syndrome. For many, it usually stops within a few weeks of leaving the holy sites.

Around 2002, our priest was transferred to another parish and replaced by another, who was, how shall I say, less than enthusiastic about his job? It was also the beginning of public awareness of the horrendous amount of sexual abuse by priests in the Church and the cover-ups that made it even worse.

The last Mass I attended was in the little church in Woodstock, Vermont. I was seated toward the back of the church, watching the obese, lazy priest as he barely participated in/led the Mass from a chair near the altar. He didn't bother with the singing. He looked bored by the proceedings.

"Body," he said as he handed me the wafer when I went up to receive Communion. Just "body," instead of the full "This is the body of Christ." The shelf was now broken. And this time it was irreparably damaged.

I was done, finally finished with the Church, with *all* organized religion. Do I miss it? No. Never. However, the lesson I learned was to separate my spirituality from *any* religion. I did miss having a spiritual community, but I found it not worth the dogma or the personalities associated with it.

Vermont, the Green Mountain State

⌒

THE NEXT MOVE WAS GOING to be across the river to Vermont, the Green Mountain State. The difference between the two states is both geological and political. New Hampshire, the Granite State, is separated from Vermont by the Connecticut River and underneath that by the Ammonoosuc Fault. Their soils are different as well, with Vermont soil being more conducive to agriculture. New Hampshire, with more cities, became more industrial. On the surface, they both looked similar, with beautiful lakes, rivers, and majestic mountains, though much higher in New Hampshire. Vermont has its sugar maples, and New Hampshire pines and white oak.

Politically, though, they are worlds apart. Vermont, being more liberal and Democratic, has more Birkenstock dealers and Bernie Sanders. New Hampshire, with a larger population, is decidedly conservative Republican, with Harley dealerships, factories, and cities. But no state income tax.

I could *feel* the difference as I crossed the Connecticut River, going back and forth between the two states. I was ready to pay more taxes just to live in Vermont! Besides, the steep, 1,500-foot driveway of our New Hampshire house was scary in the wintertime. After Ed's truck slid down on its own while he was shoveling, we decided to move. We heard later that the volunteer fire department had decided that if our house caught fire in the winter, they would just wave to us from the bottom of the driveway. And we did have a small fire in the chimney, which was, thankfully, relatively easy to put out.

There was no one to say goodbye to in New Hampshire as we moved across the river to Vermont, just as we'd had no one to say hello to when we moved there.

We chose to live in a rural setting, on a dirt road outside of Woodstock, Vermont. I did get my horse. Tiki, a Morgan gelding, joined me as soon as I got a job at the Vet Center in White River Junction, VT. But I needed to learn how to ride! Renting a horse as a teen in the Bronx for an hour or so still left me ignorant of even the basics. So I took lessons. Riding in the arena on a well-trained horse, I learned a very important truth: the instructor who had saddled the horse before I got on did not tighten the cinch enough. Walking and trotting, stopping and starting, the horse stopped, but the saddle didn't. When the saddle slipped, leaving me hanging off sideways, I thought, "I'll just let go. I'll be okay, I'm only a few feet from the ground." Wrong. Pain, severe and strong, as four ribs broke and punctured my lung. "I can't breathe," I managed to croak, which immediately and thankfully filled my lungs with needed air. I also couldn't move without severe chest pain.

An ambulance ride to the hospital, a few days of inpatient care, and then home to the best nursing care I had ever seen or had, by Nurse Ed. And a very important lesson: I am always responsible for tightening my own girth. Or in other words, *I* am responsible for the choices I do or do not make and the outcomes that result. Though I have to admit, sometimes shit happens.

By then Ed had joined me in riding, and we had two horses. We could ride them right from the barn, down the driveway, and "around the block." It was beautiful, almost heavenly to watch the seasons from the back of our horses. Northern New England, by the way, has six seasons. In addition to a six-month winter, a three-month spring/summer, and a gorgeous two-week fall, we had mud season in March and April, followed quickly by a biting-black-fly season in May.

Horses brought us closer together in a very new way. For the first time in our marriage, we had a real hobby that we both loved and shared. Now we rode together in horse heaven!

In short order, we bought a horse trailer with a small living quarters and traveled to Acadia National Park and Gettysburg to camp and ride every year. Married almost thirty years, we became even closer. Finally, the cult days were over, both in time and distance. I found that healing from trauma *can* happen, even if it takes some years. Our horses were very therapeutic for the both of us.

The Vet Center

I CIRCLED THE BUILDING, CASING the joint before I entered. It was a two-story brick building among three others in a small office park in White River Junction, Vermont. I was looking for a job, and this was the only position open for a psychotherapist within fifty miles. Though I preferred part-time work, the ad was for a full-time position as a counselor at the Vet Center. I had no idea what a Vet Center was, other than it was part of the Department of Veterans Affairs. So much for preparation for the interview.

There were two doors with Vet Center signs above them on the first floor, so I chose one and entered the large room. It looked like a fraternity clubhouse. It was about twenty by thirty feet, and it had a pool table, TV, and comfy sofas. On the walls were pictures of veterans, the Vietnam Veterans Memorial Wall in Washington, DC, a flag, and some pretty Vermont scenes. On the other side of the room was a kitchen with refrigerator, stove, sink, and table. I was impressed by its hominess and feeling of welcome and informality. It was the heart of the Vet Center, I learned.

They were waiting for me. A half-dozen Vietnam vets; the team leader, Tim Beebe; and Lance Werner, the other counselor. Staring at me. No smiles. Tim led me to his office, and so began my interview.

"Are you a vet?" was the first thing they wanted to know.

"No," I replied.

"Was anyone in your family a veteran?"

"No," I said again. "But I had two uncles who fought in World War II."

"So what makes you think you are qualified to work with Vietnam vets with post-traumatic stress disorder?"

"Well, I have worked with many PTSD clients who were sexual abuse survivors and victims of cults." I said the word "cult" and held my breath, not sure how they would react. Most people I encountered thought I must be crazy or stupid or both to have been in a cult.

"Cults?" When they asked me why I was interested in cults, I had some explaining to do. Almost reluctantly, I told them I had been in a psychotherapy cult and even written a book about recovery issues.

"Wonderful!" the team leader replied, much to my surprise. Being in a cult was almost (but not quite) as good as being a combat vet. They assumed that it must have been very traumatic (it was) and that I too had PTSD (maybe), and I was therefore acceptable to them.

A week later I got grilled by another team leader from the Burlington Vet Center as a backup. I wasn't the usual kind of person who applied. They wanted another vet, preferably with PTSD, to work there. In any case, I was happy when they told me I was their first choice for the position, as they knew that I had been in a cult and therefore must have PTSD too. I was a pseudo vet.

I learned later that they watched me circle the building a few times before I entered. That was in my favor. It was wisely noted by them—after all, they all had PTSD—that I was cautious myself, and though they wanted another vet for the position, none had applied. In fact, I was the only one who applied, even though they had been looking for someone for almost a year. They were desperate.

Earning the trust of the vets at the center was not easy. At that time, in 1994, they did not feel welcome at the Veterans Administration Medical Center (VAMC) a couple of miles away, or anywhere else for that matter. They described being shunned and looked down upon by the World War II and Korean War vets at the VA hospital as not having been in a *real* war.

I heard repeatedly of their cruel welcome home when they returned from Vietnam—being spat upon, cursed, and rejected by their peers, possible employers, schools, everywhere. They were called murderers, rapists, and baby killers, furthering their isolation. They told me how they learned to hide the fact that they had been in Vietnam, or even in the military. They were shamed by others, including their peers who had not been drafted or enlisted, which added to whatever feelings of guilt they came home with. They grew their hair long, smoked dope (which often started in Nam anyway) and tried to resemble the anti-war hippie culture. Many had problems with alcohol and drugs that began overseas, with some getting hooked on the hard stuff in order to deal with the horrors of war.

I was greeted for a long time by stares and silence as I entered the building. At the first therapy group I attended, I was grilled and looked at with hostility. Why was I here? Why did I want to work with *them*? What did I know about the Vietnam war? How did *I* feel about it and them? What did *I* do during the war?

"Well, when I graduated from nursing school in 1965, I seriously considered joining the army," I answered truthfully. I just didn't admit that I chose instead to get a dog.

"How does your husband feel about you working here? Is he afraid of us?"

Afraid? That surprised me! Why should he be afraid of *them*? I had a lot to learn about their return home after their service in Vietnam.

I was asked those things again and again. I got through it okay, but my boss made sure that my first clients were not Vietnam vets. I was assigned to veterans from other wars and eras, like Korea and WWII, until I earned their trust.

I was also told that I needed to dress down—no suits, skirts, or dresses, just jeans, sneakers, and sweaters, and I needed to play pool. He also told me, "We don't use darn as a curse word here. If you want to belong, you'll have to do better than that." Then he listed, or rather encouraged me to say, all the words I can't put in here! Easy, I thought. I can now fit in!

When I was hired, I asked if I could bring my dog to work with me. Didn't hurt to ask. My boss said sure. When I brought in Jessie, my 145-pound English mastiff, we were greeted with shocked surprise. But then she made my life a lot easier. Nothing like a big friendly lick to help even the most untrusting of my clients relax and open up. If at first they didn't like or trust me, they liked and trusted her. Dogs and vets, I quickly found, went together well. Dogs, at least my therapy dogs, were loving and open, bridging the gap between me, the newcomer nonvet, and these very wounded warriors.

Jessie was the first of my three therapy dogs followed by Indy and Raven, the two Bernese Mountain Dogs pictured above. The little dachshund, Maya, stuck behind Indy on the couch, belonged to the veteran I was counseling. Three dogs in eighteen years. All beloved, and my ticket to quicker acceptance and trust by every new vet who walked in the door.

The aura of the Vet Centers at that time was one of camaraderie. We ate together, planned annual trips to the Vietnam Veterans Memorial, had midnight vigils on Memorial Day, and took fishing trips on the Connecticut River. That meant that we spent days, nights, and weekends together annually on our travels. This was no ordinary client/therapist relationship. Some of the guys shared Thanksgiving dinner with my boss, and the lines between therapeutic relationships and friendships sometimes became a bit blurry. In those days, this was the norm here.

The twenty or so Vet Centers in the northeast section of the country had annual conferences where the latest in research and treatment for PTSD were shared with all the counselors. In the course of that week, which rotated annually from one state to another, we ate, drank, and learned together. We developed strong friendships and an esprit de corps that at first reminded me, and then replaced, my group of friends from the post-cult days.

Oh, speaking of my post-cult days, as I said, I never made much from my book, but I did have my last TV experience, on *First Edition* in 1995. I was always excited to be invited on a TV show and didn't refuse them. With permission from my boss, I took some time off from work to fly down to New York for the show—at their expense, of course. After appearing on the show, a snowstorm delayed my return for another two days.

"Cults or vets—choose!" my boss Tim ordered me, sitting me down in his office and staring hard at me.

"I'm staying here, Tim!" I responded without hesitation. There was no question about what my choice would be: it was work or no work. Income or no income. Horses or no horses.

I left the cult world behind without a glance. Or regret. This was the best job I ever had.

EMDR and Post-Traumatic Stress Disorder

⌒

I BROUGHT WITH ME TO the Vet Center my training in EMDR for the treatment of trauma. Post-traumatic stress disorder had only been recognized as a distinct disorder by the American Psychiatric Association in 1980. Soldiers were well known to be affected by war, and names for their postwar condition have included "war neurosis," "battle fatigue," and "shell shock," among others, since the Civil War and before.

I was trained in EMDR in1992, a year before I moved up north. I had used it successfully, mostly with women who were sexually abused. EMDR was then very new. Because of that, it was not allowed for use in the Vet Centers, but Tim was eager for me to use any treatment that might help those with PTSD. We just didn't tell *his* boss.

At that time, treatment for PTSD consisted of medication and supportive individual and group therapy. It quickly became apparent that EMDR was quite helpful, with good symptom reduction and relief for my clients. My office became sought after at the center, despite the EMDR prohibition. Within another five years, EMDR became better established and was named as one of the premier treatments for PTSD by the American Psychological Association, as well as by the Department of Defense and the Veterans Administration. I was ahead of the curve.

The first veteran who agreed to try out EMDR was Tom, a Vietnam army vet who came to the center for counseling. He had been transporting military supplies to a fire base that came under heavy attack after he arrived. He described being shocked and scared by the assault by the North Vietnamese troops raining firepower upon the base.

Taking part in the defense, he watched and admired as another soldier was shot and severely wounded yet got up and continued to fire his weapon. The next thing he remembered was getting shot and sitting down beneath a tree for the remainder of the engagement.

"I'm a coward. Here is this guy getting up and fighting, and all I do is sit under a tree until it's over. I'm worthless," he said, embarrassed.

For the next thirty years, he believed himself to be a coward because he didn't get up and continue fighting. And that was only the first of many traumatic events he experienced in Nam that we explored.

We started by taking a complete history. I explained carefully what we would do to desensitize the traumatic incident(s) chosen. I wanted his permission before we went back into combat—what it would look and feel like and what he could expect. Informed consent was essential, because if we were successful, he was going to go back into battle. I explained the bilateral stimulation options, which include altering eye movements, tapping, or audio tones. (Later on, he and some other vets would choose all three together).

I recorded the present negative problematic thinking, which was "I am a coward" and "I should have continued to fight," as well as how he would like to see and think about himself. He wanted to believe that he did the best he could. Of course, he currently did *not* believe that at all. His strongest negative emotions were guilt and shame, measured as a ten on a scale of zero to ten.

Tom chose to alter eye movements and followed my hand motion back and forth as he silently relived the traumatic event before me. I watched him closely, observing his eyes opening wide in fear and his respirations rapidly increasing as he went back in time.

"Oh my God! Of course I couldn't get up! I was shot in the chest!" he shouted, stopping suddenly after a few minutes of processing.

For the first time, he remembered the event fully and understood why he couldn't get up. We continued the eye movements until he was able to relax completely, and at last he truly believed and understood that he'd done the best he could. No more guilt and shame from that event. No more nightmares and intrusive thoughts of being a coward. It felt like a miracle to him. And to me too! It gave me the courage and belief that I could help these guys.

Tom continued to travel weekly to White River Junction from Massachusetts, a two-hour trip each way, and worked on the other traumas from Nam. He made it to the center in the worst of winter weather, when I didn't dare go down my own driveway. We used EMDR for his other war traumas as well, and he became my best salesman at the center. I was in business! I got the full backing of Tim and began to get many referrals for EMDR.

But I wasn't always successful. That was very evident soon afterward, when a vet got stuck reliving his trauma, and I couldn't get him unstuck.

"It's all my fault," he said bitterly. "Lou, my RT (radio telephone operator) and I were walking point ahead of our platoon, and we were ambushed. He fell on top of me, and I pretended to be dead. I should have known we were going to be attacked."

I didn't know enough or have enough experience to help him through his trauma. He lost his best friend and felt helpless and guilty. I was determined to learn more. I'd had only the first part of EMDR training. So I did the only thing I could: I continued training in EMDR and eventually became an approved consultant and even facilitated at EMDR trainings around the country.

Doing trauma work meant getting intimately involved in the horrors of war. Sitting closely by the vets, near their couch or chair, I listened and worked through each massacre, death of comrades, death of women and children, and even rape of civilians. Through the traumas, Jessie, followed by Indy and Raven, offered silent, nonjudgmental support as well, sitting near my clients.

As they talked, for the next eighteen years, I imagined traveling with them on patrols through the jungles during the monsoon season, slogging through mud, soaking wet, exhausted and hungry. Even without the rain, with the temperature and humidity around a hundred, it was unbearable, especially while carrying sixty-five-pound backpacks filled with ammo and some MREs (meals ready to eat). With sodden socks that seemed to disintegrate with wear, they had bunions, painful sores, infections, and callouses on their feet. They were bitten by bugs of all kinds and learned to examine their boots before putting them on—that is, if they ever took them off. Spiders, centipedes, and millipedes, sometimes two feet long, were omnipresent. Tarantulas the size of dinner plates hurt like hell when they bit. Poisonous and constrictor snakes, gigantic rats, and even tigers were feared and avoided.

On patrol, they were alert—no, hyperalert—for any signs of the enemy lying in wait to ambush and kill. I accompanied them through attacks by the Communist Viet Cong and North Vietnamese troops.

I watched when, horribly wounded, they were the sole survivors of their units, bleeding among their dead and dying friends. They distrusted the newbies, the newly arrived soldiers, who, through inexperience, accidentally drew enemy fire, endangering all. Worse were the new lieutenants who ordered them, through ignorance or incompetence, into dangerous combat areas.

I listened to the harrowing accounts of helicopters being shot down, surviving ambushes and assaults, being medevacked to hospitals and MASH units. I went underground with Adam, a "tunnel rat." His job was to destroy the tunnels the Viet Cong dug throughout Vietnam, tunnels where they stored arms, food, and even had bunkers and hospitals. Secured by rope, those above ground could haul him out, alive or dead. Tunnel rats, chosen for their relatively small size, were admired for their bravery and sent wherever needed. His worst incident was encountering an enemy soldier in the dark narrow tunnels and fighting for his life, armed only with a knife. When he finally emerged, he was cheered by those who pulled him out, wounded.

"You know, I didn't feel any fear going down into the tunnels, not until I came home. Then flashbacks and nightmares made me wonder how I did it all," said Adam. We worked through those fears successfully with EMDR as I relived his tour with him.

Several vets needed to deal with their guilt of killing civilians. One

Vietnam vet talked about shooting a small child who came running to him. He didn't know why he did it, only that he shot him, reflexively. A father now himself, this horrified and haunted him ever since.

During the processing of the incident, he recalled seeing a friend get killed when he went to pick up a crying toddler. "I watched when Vic bent down, the kid raised his arms to be picked up, and the grenades placed under his armpits by the Vietcong exploded, killing them both." Shocked and horrified, he had forgotten that. Only while reprocessing did the whole event make sense and he could forgive himself.

Another vet described his guilt and anguish while serving with his unit in Kosovo, doing crowd control.

"Hold your fire, men," instructed his lieutenant, the officer in charge, as the angry mob swarmed toward them. Despite his orders, my client shot a young teen. What he suddenly remembered while doing EMDR was that he had tripped, falling backward, and his gun went off. Seeing what happened, his LT sharply repeated, "Forget about it!" And my client did. He forgot that the shooting was accidental.

One of my favorite vets—okay, I admit to having some favorites among all these courageous men—was Leon, a true Southern gentleman haunted by the memory of causing the death of an elderly woman. Throughout the many years that I knew him, he never failed to call me ma'am. It was hard for him to just say Mady.

He related that upon entering the village, an elderly woman came up to him and offered him a bowl of food. Not hungry, he said, "No, thank you, ma'am" and refused. Then, when she continued to insist, following him and pushing the bowl up against him, his annoyance turned to anger. "No! *You* eat it!" he finally ordered. He then watched her convulse and die as she ate the food meant for him. *His fault, his guilt.* It was very difficult for him to absolve himself of that death. Reliving that event repeatedly through the years, he continued to wonder if it would have been better for him to have eaten it himself and died.

Over and over again, I listened as these courageous men were faced with horrendous choices. Choices that haunted them for decades.

Choices that had no good answers or solutions. Thankfully, many times I could help them through them. Sadly, there were times I could not.

Secondary PTSD was well known by this time. Family and counselors of those traumatized often suffered some PTSD as well—sleep difficulties, intrusive thoughts, and so on. I think what helped me is that I went through not only the traumas they survived, but also the relief and healing that the therapy provided. During the reliving, I almost felt like I was there too, with them. I felt the horror and pain, shame and guilt they were feeling, but I was also shielded at the same time. I had faith that walking with them through their pain, we could get through it together.

I believe that perhaps through helping to heal others, I was also healed. Hmmm. On second thought, they were *all* my favorites.

9/11 and the Team

View of Twin Towers aflame from the New Jersey side of the Hudson River
Photo by Wally Gobetz

Rick was my first scheduled appointment that morning, and he had only started to describe his difficulties at home when a frantic knock on the door stopped him midsentence. It was 8:55 a.m. I had *never* gotten interrupted in session before.

"Come out, come out *now*! See what's on TV!"

Startled, worried, and a bit confused, we rushed out to the waiting room to see what was going on. I saw gathered around the TV a dozen vets and staff watching as the news repeatedly showed American Airlines Flight 11 crashing into the ninety-sixth floor of the North Tower of the World Trade Center only a few minutes before, at 8:46 a.m. I couldn't think. I was numb. It was incomprehensible to me how it could be an accident!

We looked on, frozen in front of the set, wondering how this could be happening here. The TV news stations showed the crash over and over again.

As if to prove it was no accident, at 9:03 a.m., as we were watching, a second plane, United Airlines Flight 175, crashed into the eightieth floor of the South Tower. There was a deadly silence in the room as we all grappled with what we had just witnessed. I heard comments like, "Oh my God, not again!" "We're at war!" "Oh God, oh God, oh God." "Where is it going to be next?"

And then, "I hope we're safe in Vermont!"

The TV mesmerized all of us. Shock, fear, and incredible rage do not begin to describe the horror I and the others felt.

"Oh my God!" we cried as we saw desperate trapped men and women jumping, falling, or being blown out of the top floors.

At 9:32 we saw the damage to the Pentagon by American Airlines Flight 77.

At 10:00 a.m. the South Tower of the World Trade Center collapsed upon itself from the top, caving into the bottom. Following it less than a half hour later, the North Tower collapsed as well. Unbelievable!

At 10:06, we learned that United Flight 93 had crashed in Pennsylvania, possibly en route to Washington, DC.

"I need to pray, please," said Rick, a devout Catholic, and together we prayed the rosary in my office. The rest of the day was shot. The only thing on TV was the attacks, shown repeatedly.

Shellshocked, we watched the news until it was time to go home. I can only imagine what was going on in the hearts and minds of those veterans. They were mostly silent, in their own hells. In all our minds, we were no longer safe here at home. New York City, Washington, DC, and Pennsylvania. Where next? Our country was no longer invulnerable to attack or war. This was a huge turning point in our history. Not since Pearl Harbor had any nation or people dared to strike us with such impunity. But then, with PTSD, safety *never* exists.

We were very busy the next couple of weeks as all of us attempted to come to grips with the attacks. The vets were retraumatized. The uncertainty of the future was on all their minds. Their PTSD was highly magnified. Hypervigilance, nightmares, and intrusive thoughts, as well as numbness and survivor guilt. Old wounds, deaths of comrades, and attacks and ambushes were revivified. Anger flared.

I checked with my family in NYC to make sure they were safe, and I could feel their fear and anger too. I had been there only a month before for my nephew's wedding at a hotel only a couple of blocks from the Towers. You couldn't miss seeing them, the tallest of the skyscrapers. This was my city too. I had lived in New York City for the first twenty-two years of my life, the last five in Manhattan.

I heard about some family members losing friends in the attacks on the towers. Their anger as well as fear boiled over. Now that I was living safely up north, I was treated almost as an outsider.

"It wasn't you who were attacked! You were safe. But it could have been any of us here!" Were they wrong? I wondered.

The Department of Veterans Affairs then stepped into action. In coordination with the Regional Directors of the Readjustment Counseling Service offices, I was recruited to go down to NYC with a select task force to debrief the staff of the NYC and New Jersey Vet Centers and VA medical centers. I didn't hesitate for a second to say yes.

My first team leader, Tim, now working at the regional HQ, knew that I was a disaster mental health volunteer with the American Red Cross. He had given approval for me to work with them in Vermont in events such as plane crashes, ice storms, and floods. I am sure it was he who recommended me for this role in NYC.

There were five of us. The other three counselors were from Vet Centers in Florida, West Virginia, and Alaska. I felt very honored to be part of this group. Accompanying us was an assistant director of the Readjustment Counseling Services from Washington, DC. Our task was to do critical incident stress debriefing, or CISD, with large groups of employees at the VA medical centers within sight of the attacks. CISD was developed for use with small groups as a supportive crisis intervention immediately following trauma events. This was now two or three weeks after the attack. But no one had *ever* anticipated the need for this kind of intervention before.

Manhattan

I DROVE DOWN TO NEW York City in our Vet Center government van so that we could easily gain access to the places and sites we were to visit. The other team members were flying into New York from around the country. As I drew nearer to the city, I kept scanning the skyline for the towers, which were no longer visible. I was not surprised, just sad.

Joining the others that first afternoon, we greeted each other warmly and got to know one another. Our first stop was lower Manhattan to view what remained of the Twin Towers. Nothing. It was now almost three weeks after the attack. The air and streets had been mostly cleared of debris. The soot and chemicals released by the crashing towers had been mostly cleansed by the sanitation department, assisted by wind and rain. But there was still smoke in the sky ahead of us as we got closer.

The streets were blocked off to traffic, and the area around the (former) World Trade Center was fenced off from onlookers for several blocks around the site. We were given permission to enter in the government car. It felt weird to drive down Manhattan streets that were empty of traffic. We approached slowly, alone with our thoughts.

The ruins were still smoldering. The rubble continued to burn and, I learned later, would continue to burn for another three months.

It was hard to make sense of what happened. Severe cognitive dissonance. Instead of the solid Manhattan I used to know, with one building rising next to another separated only by narrow side streets, there was just a giant hole. For several blocks in diameter were the crumbling remains of the completely leveled buildings.

World Trade Center

Rescue workers continue their efforts Monday, Sept. 24, 2001, at the site of the Sept. Center terrorist attack in New York. (AP Photo/Ted S. Warren, Pool)

Much of the ruins had already been carted off. In Mitchell Zuckoff's book *Fall and Rise: The Story of 9/11*, I learned that of the 2,753 victims, men, women, and children, there were few body parts that were identifiable. However, in those tons of cement and steel, twenty-one thousand fragments of the victims, some almost microscopic in size, were salvaged for later identification, which would take years.

We sat down for dinner that night in a lovely outdoor Italian restaurant to do some needed debriefing of ourselves. We were far from immune to the horror we had just seen.

"How are you feeling?" we asked each other, comparing and verbalizing the shock and horror we had just witnessed. (Have I said shock and horror enough so far?)

The next day we toured the temporary emergency centers on the piers of the Hudson River. There, the Federal Emergency Management Administration, the American Red Cross, and other state and federal agencies had the humongous task of helping families locate and discover the fate of their family and friends and receive assistance. Some who lived close to the World Trade Center had severe damage to their housing and businesses.

It was here that I first saw the hundreds—no, thousands of posters peppered across Manhattan saying things like, "*MISSING!*" And then below was a picture (usually smiling) of their husband or wife, father or mother, son or daughter or friend. I could feel the pain and desperation in their search. I was overwhelmed by the sheer numbers of these flyers on walls, fences, cars, and windows throughout Manhattan.

Our first counseling task was to visit the Vet Center in the Federal Building in Manhattan. At the entrance we were searched for weapons. And the guards were deadly serious.

We traveled up the elevator to the Vet Center near the top floor. Jack, the team leader, gave us a tour and showed us the windows that had a direct view of the Towers only a few blocks away.

"Here is where we watched the Towers get hit and fall," he said quietly. Stunned, I stared out that window, trying to imagine what he saw that morning. We sat down and listened to their story as they talked about their feelings then and now. Shock, fear, and anger.

A very familiar scenario was repeated at the Newark Vet Center, where my good friend Jane Harris, a psychologist, worked. The culture of the Vet Center is one of support, and I knew these counselors well from our annual conferences.

"Thanks for coming! It's great that you came down," she said. I think they appreciated our support and concerns, and that the Veterans Administration cared enough to send us.

It was another story at the Lyons and Orange Veterans Administration Medical Centers, both in New Jersey. From their windows too, they could view the attacks occurring across the Hudson River. We spent the next few days with hundreds of employees on all three shifts. Together we "debriefed" groups of thirty to fifty staff members during the day, afternoon, and evening hours. It was impossible to talk with them individually or listen to all their experiences.

I came away from that week thinking it was mostly a waste of time. We were too late. Three weeks had now passed, and the people we talked to, especially at the hospitals, were *very* angry. Much of this was displaced onto us, as we were outsiders who could not appreciate what they had gone through. We were not New Yorkers (and I had left). Even the New Jersey employees stated very clearly that "they were New Yorkers too!"

I left NYC and wondered, Did I help anyone at all? Did doing CISD with large groups of people, so long after the attacks, help? I was certain we were too little, too late. I then remembered a saying from the Talmud:

> Whoever destroys a single life is considered by Scripture to have destroyed the whole world, and whoever saves a single life is considered by Scripture to have saved the whole world.
>
> —The Talmud

I was sure that I didn't save any lives, but I hoped I had helped to make at least one person feel better.

Women Are Veterans Too!

In 2004, the Veterans Health Administration coined the term "military sexual trauma," MST for short. As I had already started treating women veterans, and sexual trauma had been my specialty area prior to joining the Vet Center, I officially became the Military Sexual Trauma specialist, in addition to treating combat vets. I had also been treating the few male veterans who came forward with sexual trauma as well.

I began a therapy group for women vets with military sexual trauma. Not only did we meet weekly, but we had arts and crafts workshops, and (therapeutic) horseback riding was added at a nearby riding facility. We also took an overnight trip to Washington, DC, to visit the Women in Military Service for America Memorial and museums.

When one of the women suggested a trip to ride the rapids on the Hudson River, they were all gung ho. Permission and funding for the trip were immediately granted!

Taking the Vet Center van, it was large enough to fit all of us, and our equipment, food, and personal gear. We had two tents, and yes, I roomed with them in one of them. This is something I never would have considered in private practice, but it was quickly given approval by our team leader.

Setting up our tents in the campground, we laughed and joked and did some craftwork provided by the group members. Together we barbecued dinners, told stories, and shared feelings of friendship and respect. And we had fun!

At the river, our tour guides equipped us with wet suits and life jackets. We were handed our paddles and instructed by two guides, one in the front and one in the back of the raft, down the rapids. It was both scary and exciting! Together our group bonded even more strongly as we shared a sense of accomplishment and mastery of our fears. These vets were a joy to work and be with.

Fire!

VET CENTER STAFF WORKED CLOSELY with the VAMC less than a mile away in White River Junction. We attended in-service meetings there, and psychiatrists came to the Center for medical checks with our veterans, who were on a variety of meds for PTSD. We also received weekly consultations with them at the Center. Our vets were therefore comfortable with both service providers utilizing a variety of medical services. It was not unusual for vets to be referred to one or the other for a good fit.

One such referral was a woman vet whom I treated for about one year and then referred back to the VAMC for continuing care, as she no longer met our requirements for treatment. (Due to HIPPA requirements, I cannot add anything more about this client.) She did not want to go back to the VAMC for continued care and ended *all* treatment against medical advice.

A couple of months later, someone broke into my new horse trailer, tore up the mattress in the living quarters, and smeared paint on the walls. I called the police, who investigated without any results. I found a cigarette lighter on the floor of the shed. No fire damage, but suspicious. None of us smoked. I didn't want to think about who could have done this. But I knew who was guilty.

Weeks later I learned that at around the same time, someone had entered the VA hospital's employee parking lot and, using a baseball bat, caused over $4,000 worth of damage to cars. The VA police saw the perpetrator in the act, but to my surprise, she was neither apprehended nor charged. They knew who she was and did nothing!

~~~

Now it was my turn, *again*. The dirt road leading to our house was dark until I got to the flashing lights of the police cars, which blocked it. They said the road was closed, then asked where I was heading. I told them my address, and they grimly waved me on. They did not tell me why the road was closed. This was like a nightmare scene from a scary movie. I had with me my Bernese Mountain dogs, Indy and Raven, who both worked with me at the Vet Center that day.

Dazed and frightened, I continued up the road until I got to my driveway. Flashing emergency and fire truck lights led all the way up to the house.

The police, firemen, and Ed were waiting for me. You couldn't see any damage outside the home, but once the door was open, everything inside was black. With flashlights, I could see the walls, ceilings, and furniture. There was smoke damage everywhere and the smell of burnt everything. Ed was in shock, and so was I. He hugged me as he described what he saw when he came home a short while ago.

The police stood silently by as I witnessed the destruction caused by the fire. When they asked me if I knew who might have done this, I had no doubt. When I told them, I was surprised and relieved when they said she was already in custody. I then had to explain to them how I knew her.

My fire was the third she started that day. The first was a judge's home, across the river in New Hampshire. It burned to the ground and killed her cat. No one was at home, and her relationship to that person was unknown, if she even had any. The next house was up the road from me. They related that when she knocked on the door, no one answered, and she just walked in. Lots of unlocked doors in Vermont! What she didn't know was that there was someone in the house upstairs who ignored the knock. Hearing some noises downstairs, he came down and saw her setting fires in the kitchen and living room. When she saw him, she ran outside. I was told he grabbed her by the arm, and she said, "Don't touch me, I am crazy." When she jerked away from him, she ran to her truck and quickly drove away, but not before he got her license plate number and called the police.

When she got to my house, she broke a basement window and entered. She rummaged through my drawers, our belongings, and clothes. I don't know if she took anything, but all my jewelry was still there. She saw my two kittens and my parrot before going down to the basement and setting the fires that destroyed the interior of my home and killed my precious friends.

When I asked about our pets, Ed showed me, tears rolling down his face, where he had placed our two dear ragdoll kittens, Mike and Milly, and my beloved African Gray parrot, Simon. I'd had Simon thirteen years, since he was a baby. He was baby bird and I was mommy bird to him. With a vocabulary of over two hundred words and sentences, which he always used appropriately, he was like another child to me.

The contents of the house were destroyed, but nothing equaled the loss of those three special beings. Thankfully, she left the horses in the barn alone. They were big, and she was probably afraid of them.

I was filled with rage at her. I wasn't even this angry at Chase. For months afterward, I imagined her coming up the driveway and ripping her apart with my bare hands. I wouldn't even choose to shoot her. I imagined destroying her slowly, piece by piece. Another psychopath in my life. When would I ever learn?

Johnna Dana, who lived across the street from us, graciously invited us to live with her until we could find temporary housing. Another friend boarded our horses. Johnna was my best friend in VT. Together Ed, Johnna and I rode our horses through the dirt roads and trails around our home. She was almost as traumatized as us by the arson.

Our insurance company was great and helped us organize and recover/repair what we could. With over $200,000 in damages it took 3-4 months to have the house ready for occupancy. We found a temporary home to rent while our builder rebuilt the inside of our home—walls, plumbing, wiring. In three months, it was literally new again, and we could move back in. Nothing was going to drive us from this home that we loved. With fresh paint, new furniture, and new clothes, we began again. But I never got another parrot.

The investigations and the trial were exhausting and took months. The publicity and the questioning, the suspicions and the finger point-ing…how could this have happened? I was relieved when she was found guilty and received a prison sentence.

When she was released less than a year later, she had an ankle brace-let and restraining order, which kept her several miles from me.

I don't hate her anymore. Hate has been replaced by pity. She has had a horrible life, and I cannot imagine any improvement in her men-tal condition in this lifetime. She, too, I turn over to God for forgiveness. I am also glad I now live far away from her.

Lesson learned: there are *no* earthly possessions that are important. They can all be replaced if necessary. But nothing can replace the loss of those we love, pets or people.

Rest in peace, Simonbird, Mikey and Milly.

Angels to the Rescue!

⟜⟶

It was a hot August day in 1986 in Connecticut. My friend Beth and I rented a couple of horses and went for a ride. After an hour in the heat, we returned to the stables, dismounted, and walked our horses to cool them off. We were all sweaty in the hot, humid weather that afternoon.

"Great ride!" Beth said, leading her horse ahead, followed (too) closely by me and mine.

Suddenly, her horse kicked back forcefully at my horse and me with both hind legs. Within nanoseconds, my horse reared up and over me! Without time to think, I threw myself away from their deadly hooves with a Chinese roll learned in kung fu. It saved my life. When I got up, I saw, perhaps twenty feet away, a brown-robed monk, watching and smiling at me.

"Who is that?" I asked myself in amazement. I blinked, and he was gone. I was shaken but unhurt.

"Did you see him, Beth? The monk!" I shouted to her. My guardian angel!

"No. Where?" she asked, confused. She didn't see him, but she heartily agreed I was lucky to be alive.

⟜⟶

EMDR immersed me in the trauma of war as well as sexual assault. Going into battle, witnessing first hand death and destruction, bravery, and even cowardice for almost eighteen years, gave me an appreciation (?) of the horrors and the uselessness of war. I admired the choices, courage, and pain the veterans carried with them, often for decades, following their service to our country.

Though I was no longer a practicing Catholic, prayer was still part of my life. While working through the most intense part of desensitizing trauma, I often said a Hail Mary to myself. It seemed to help both me and my clients. To my shock and surprise, three times during those years, during my prayers, clients revealed visions of Mother Mary and angels caring for them during the worst part of the trauma processing. They explained that the vision was accompanied by resolution of the trauma, relief, and peace.

Dick Chase, a marine corporal, told me what happened as we prepared to desensitize the incident when he got wounded the day he was the sole survivor of an attack.

"I was ordered by my lieutenant to take my guys up along the river and meet up with him and the other troops on the other side of the ridge. I started to argue with him. I said, 'That's crazy! That route is known to have VC scattered throughout! It's a death trap!' He looked right at me and threatened court martial if I disobeyed. So what choice did I have? If I refused, I would be immediately sent back to base, my men would get another leader, and they would still be ordered to follow a stupid command."

Taking a deep breath, he continued. "So I followed orders. They trusted and depended upon me. We didn't get very far. Halfway there, we were attacked, and they were all killed. All but me. It's my fault. I should have done something different."

Wracked with guilt, he began the desensitization of the attack. Like so many others, Dick went deeply into the memory, accompanied by the fear, horror, and guilt. Jolting out of the event, he exclaimed, "Of course, I couldn't have done anything else. We were surrounded on all sides by the NVA!" (the North Vietnamese Army.) He then drew me a diagram of the attack, showing his dozen men and himself surrounded by hundreds of NVA soldiers.

We then continued to his rescue. Heaped onto the pile of bodies with the others, he somehow alerted them that he was still alive.

"I was shot in the chest and gut. I was covered with me and Pete's blood. I guess I looked as dead as everyone else." They quickly took Dick to the nearest medical unit for emergency treatment of his wounds. He was sure he was going to die.

After this, when he was ready, we reprocessed, with EMDR, the emergency care he'd received in the MASH unit. He remembered it vividly for the first time since coming home. As he was being prepared for anesthesia, he said, "Then I saw her, the most beautiful woman I had ever seen. She stayed with me until I went into surgery and told me I would be okay."

What surprised him was that when he told the docs and medics about her, and wanted to thank her, they all laughed at him and said, "There aren't any woman here!" So what did he see?

We were doing EMDR when he remembered this. Seeing her again now, during the reprocessing, was just as special as seeing her then. He now accepted that he had been watched over by an angel.

When I asked Dick for permission to tell his story, he said, "I am glad to share it with other vets so they know that it is possible to heal from their combat experiences."

I then asked him how it felt to read this, and he responded, "At first I had a couple of bad dreams, but then that disappeared. I am very happy to remember that I have an angel watching over me!" More about Dick later.

I was working with another client who had returned to school after the war and was now a practicing attorney. As a noncombatant in Vietnam, he was bothered not so much by the military issues as by his childhood sexual abuse by a teacher. He had never disclosed this to anyone before. His anxiety prior to reprocessing was profound, and I said a silent Hail Mary.

During reprocessing, he remembered the assault vividly, and then he told me with awe, "The Blessed Mother came to me just now and told me I would be okay. It was not my fault!" He was awestruck and felt much relief and was comforted. I did not tell him about my prayers. I was awestruck as well.

A severely traumatized woman veteran related how she had been suicidal during and after her multiple and serious wounds were being treated. She been attacked physically and sexually by several men after she reported an assault of another woman by one of the men to her superiors. After weeks in the hospital in San Diego, recovering from surgery and broken bones, she no longer wished to live.

"I headed for the beach, knowing this was going to be the end. I walked into the water until the waves were over my head and my feet no longer touched the sand. I wanted to drown out all the pain and horror." But instead of dying, she was amazed when a young man swam to her and carried her safely back to the shore.

"He gently put me down on the beach, then completely disappeared!" She realized it was not yet time for her to die, that she had more to do and live for in this lifetime.

Larry, another Vietnam veteran, wrote the following:

"Some years ago, the subject of angels and their intercession on our behalf came up in a conversation. Mady asked me to share experiences I've had that have remained as profound events, such that I'm convinced some entity or benevolent presence has acted to advise and at times protect me from harm. The following are three examples that have remained crystal clear throughout my life. I make no claims to explain or have particular knowledge of why, who, or how these events occurred. What I can state with certainty and clarity is that these events are true and were not influenced by any suggestion before or after they happened. The fact is, I never discussed any of them until speaking with

Mady, after which I began to realize how, in many instances throughout my life, subtle guiding advice has been influential at crucial times.

"I was born shortly after WWII. There was a housing shortage due to all the returning GIs. We lived at that time in a run-down three-apartment tenement in a very poor section of Boston. Our apartment was on the first floor; an aunt and uncle lived across the street on the third floor of their building, and another aunt and uncle lived next to us.

"Sundays were always family day and were usually spent sharing dinner and being together. One particular Sunday, when I was about four years old, we had just come home from church, and I remember it was a fine May spring day. My father and my uncle Ed were standing on the curb talking while I was impatiently pulling at my father's sleeve to go across the street so I could visit my aunt Rose. The more I squirmed, the tighter my dad's grip on my shoulder.

"Not able to be still, I waited for him to be distracted, and before long I saw my chance. As I was about to pull free, I noticed a large red moving truck coming down our street. I hesitated, but then, thinking I could make it across, I pulled free and ran out into the street. My little legs somehow made the distance seem wider, and I froze midway. The truck was now almost on top of me when, for whatever reason, I lurched forward.

"I heard the horn and watched in slow motion as the huge grille of that truck bore down only feet away. I froze, waiting to be hit. Suddenly I felt someone grab my shoulder and pull me back just as the truck jammed his brakes. I had been square in the path of that truck and would surely have been hit. As it was, the fender grazed my face, breaking my nose. The truck driver drove my father with me in his lap to the children's hospital, where I was treated and sent home to a very grateful mother and family! To this day I still recall that grip on my shoulder pulling me from tragedy.

"At age six we had moved to a wonderful old two-family Victorian home in the Cambridge area. Our house was on a well-kept street off a main avenue. At the corner where it met the avenue was a little store known in those days as a spa. My mother that summer had allowed me to go there on errands for her on occasion. Her instructions always included staying on our side of the street and not speaking to strangers. My reward for these errands was a penny or two for the candy Mr. Marshall had on hand to choose from. One day, mother sent me to get a loaf of bread with the same cautions.

"On my way home, I stopped here and there to look at the sidewalk for pennies or watch a car go by. As I was on my way, a large black sedan slowed and pulled toward the curb. Lowering the passenger window, a well-dressed man asked, 'Little boy, do you know where number 123 is on this street?' I replied that it must be farther down past our house, which was number 93. He said, 'You've been such a helpful boy. I'll give you a ride home.' I told him no and that I really wasn't supposed to talk to strangers. He next opened the door and held out a dollar bill for me as a reward for helping. A whole dollar would buy lots of candy, I thought!

"As I reached for that dollar and my hand was just inches away, that same hand grabbed my shoulder, yanked me back onto the sidewalk and whispered in my head to run home and not look back. I told my mother, and she called the police, then gave me a good talking to. Years later she told me the police had picked that man up several streets over from ours. He was convicted of harming and molesting several children in the area. Once again, as I impulsively gave in to my own actions, some entity had pulled me from danger and instructed me to run to safety.

"In my late twenties, my wife and I were living in a rural area far west of Boston. I was working as a heating technician and was driving to a no-heat call. As I was driving, not thinking of anything in particular, a vision of my father's face appeared in front of me very briefly but so clearly I could see a sad, sorrowful look I'll never forget. Then, as the vision left, a voice spoke clearly: 'Your father is going to die soon. You'll need to be there for your mother and spend time with him.'

"My father and I were very close. I was blessed to have had a great relationship with him growing up. Several months after this happened, my father was diagnosed with cancer. He was operated on, and things looked good. Four years later he passed after a very tough time of suffering.

During those years I made every effort to be the best son I could be for us both. I think the fact I was prepared for this helped me come to terms with his loss and appreciate our last years together.

"I'm seventy-one years old, and these particular events have never lost their clarity of detail. If anything, my sense of just how profound their meaning is on many levels has only increased. I learned long ago to accept and trust there are forces or entities that intercede on our behalf should we open ourselves to being aware of our own ability to hear them. I don't have any explanation or name for them, but I know I'm watched over and am thankful."

Insomnia and PTSD

⌒

Sleep issues are commonplace among those with PTSD. Learning from my own childhood fears in the night, I used the same techniques to help others.

One vet talked about being sexually abused in an orphanage early in childhood. He said he dreaded going to bed, remembering the male attendant who would assault him at night. He still had nightmares about it.

"If you could choose any animal to sleep by your bed and protect you, what would it be?" I asked him.

After thinking about it for a moment, he said, "I want a gorilla! He doesn't have to attack him, just scare him away."

"Okay. I want you to picture him by your bedside while you go to sleep. Can you give this new friend a name?"

"Yep. Brody!" he said, smiling. I then had him "see" himself going to sleep and having that gorilla keep him safe.

He reported back to me that it worked, and he was sleeping better.

Another vet, while recuperating after surgery at the Bethesda Naval Hospital, was well enough to take a walk on the hospital grounds. To her horror, she was raped one night. Already weakened and vulnerable, she had no memory of the assault, but she was still afraid to sleep at night. Like me, she chose a black panther to be her guardian. It worked well and lessened her fear.

Dogs and Horses
for Heroes

⌣⌐

ANIMALS ARE SOME OF THE best treatments for PTSD. In addition to my therapy dogs, Jesse, Indy, and Raven, vets brought in their German shepherds, dachshunds, huskies, Chihuahuas, and mutts. Parrots and cockatiels too! All got along well. All were welcomed. I was never surprised at how good they were at lowering the anxiety and depression levels of people with PTSD. They sat by their buddies' sides on the couches or by their feet. Though they're officially recognized now as emotional support and therapy animals, who knew then that they would later be widely promoted as an essential treatment for PTSD and other disabilities?

After one vet, Terri, learned on Facebook that I was going to be writing this book, she wrote this to me, hoping I would include her story as well:

"Whenever I was struggling, just being able to pet and love on Raven as you and I worked through my therapy sessions was a huge help. If I came in upset or stressed out, she could read me and know exactly what I needed during that session, whether to lie at my feet or, if I was really struggling, to jump up on the couch to snuggle up with me. She was an excellent therapy dog!

"I was just glad I was able (and honored that she allowed me) to return the favor by doing Reiki on her when she struggled. I remember the time I came in and she wouldn't come out as she normally did to greet me, and you told me you had made her an appointment for vet care with acupuncture for her hips. So I did Reiki on her, not knowing how she would respond. As I was treating her, she leaned into me, letting me know in her own way that she knew I was trying to help alleviate her pain and heal her. The amazing thing was when she jumped up to say goodbye to me when I left my therapy session that day!

"It made my day to help her after all she had done for my sanity over the years of therapy with you and her. You told me you saved money because you didn't need to take her in for the acupuncture treatment after all. It made me happy to be able to return a small gift for all that you helped me with throughout the years.

"Thank you for your guidance and advice and treatment throughout the years. Every time I see a Bernese Mountain dog, I and smile and think lovingly of how much Raven touched my heart and the huge impact she had on my life.—DTC (FMF) Terri L. Munsey-Ballou, USN, Retired."

Later she added, "I forgot to tell you, but after you and Raven left [the Vet Center], my dog Duffy, who was a Jack Russell terrier, became my therapy dog. He really was in touch with all my emotions, not just my anxiety. It is so amazing at how well dogs and some cats (my daughter Rose's cat, Oliver, has since taken over where Duffy left off) really know how to comfort someone with anxiety issues."

Not only dogs and cats, but horses too. It started with my Tennessee Walking Horses. I became involved with the New England Tennessee Walking Horse Association and with Diane Lashoones, a physical therapist who operates Rhythm of the Rein, a therapeutic riding program. In my usual style, I jumped right in, taking a course in horse therapy, becoming involved in her program, and helping to start, with her, the newly recognized Horses for Heroes program at the local VAMC and Vet Center. It was a big hit!

We began with the Vietnam vets and then added my women veterans' group. I watched as their fear and trepidation of these huge animals changed to warmth, respect, and affection. I saw how these loving animals patiently stood still as they were brushed, tacked up, and then mounted by fearful, emotionally wounded adults. Already familiar with children with disabilities, these beautiful creatures adapted to the vets wonderfully. Though the riders were fearful and timid at first, I watched in admiration as they gained in confidence and self-respect, mastering their fears and beginning to enjoy their relationships with horses.

One of my clients, Dick, whose story has already been told in this chapter, was initially so frightened and immobilized on horseback that we each walked closely by his side as we led the horse around the indoor arena. Within weeks, that changed. After riding for a month or so, he began volunteering at the therapeutic riding center himself, and he even bought his own horse!

Dogs, horses, cats, and parrots were matches made in heaven. Is it any wonder that dog spelled backward is God?

PTSD? Me?

I HAVE OFTEN BEEN ASKED if I myself had PTSD. Looking back over the years, I can easily recall many traumatic incidents that caused sleepless nights and intrusive thoughts: in hell when smoking pot; the ten years in a cult; multiple horse accidents with ambulance and helicopter trips to the hospital; the fire. However, the one incident that troubled me the most was that day in the hospital over fifty years ago, being part of an abortion procedure and not being able to save that baby's life. I had made the choice to participate in her labor, and then when I tried to save her life, that choice was taken from me.

I believe that all these incidents in the past helped me in working through the traumas of war with veterans. As I worked to help heal others, I was also healing myself.

We all make choices, good ones as well as bad ones. Then we find out afterward, too late, that we should have made the other choice. Or perhaps we are relieved we made the "right" choice. For veterans, it may be the choice to enlist or not, or to go to Canada instead of Vietnam.

We are always making choices as we walk through each day. Some are simple ones, such as what to eat or wear, while others are more complex, what job to take, whom to date or whom to marry, whether to have kids. We don't always know which choices are dangerous and which will affect us the rest of our lives. For example, did you know that your eating choices might increase the odds of developing diabetes, high blood pressure, cancer, and Alzheimer's? We also don't know which events will severely affect the rest of our lives: illness, death of loved ones, war, drunk drivers, or climate change, to name a few. But I have come to believe that what befalls us, good and bad, are all opportunities to learn and grow.

⟵⟶

I worked at the Vet Center from 1994 to 2012. It was so much more than a job. It was a privilege and an honor to work with this incredible population for eighteen years. My coworkers were very special to me as well. I was glad I got a "second chance" to go to Vietnam. But I was also looking forward to retirement and moving south, not farther north.

At my farewell party at the Center, I was given this flag and made an honorary veteran. It was the best gift I could have ever received from my vets.

Every Tree
Every tree, every growing thing as it grows, says this truth:
"You harvest what you sow. With life as short as a half-taken breath,
don't plant anything but love."
Rumi

Part 5

Retirement and Back to the New Age

She welcomed me and told me: I am the Grandmother Tree. Come. See me, and feel my roots growing deeply beneath you. I am old, 350 years old. I have been shattered by the elements, yet I continue to grow and thrive. Parts of me are dead and dying, while new sprouts and branches thrive.

Some parts of your world are dying, yet some will survive. We will outlive your species, if you all die. You have no respect for life or each other. It is very sad. We grieve for you.

—Osage orange tree, October 13, 2014

Horses, Angels,
and Helicopters

Is RETIREMENT REALLY THE FINAL chapter of my life? We moved down to northwestern Virginia from Vermont to be near Allison, her husband, Doug, and my only grandchild, Luke, in June 2012. I had just turned sixty-six and Ed sixty-eight. We brought with us our two Tennessee Walking Horses, Gray Man and Curly, as well as my retired Morgan for Luke to ride. Raven, our elderly Bernese Mountain Dog, and four cats accompanied us as well.

On almost six acres of open field, among farmland, on a lovely, scenic rural road with views of the Blue Ridge Mountains, we built our home and put up the barn. The sounds of chickens clucking and cows mooing were heard on all sides. We loved it.

We joined two riding clubs, met people, and settled into our retirement. We volunteered at a therapeutic riding facility. Horses were a big part of our life now, and Ed and I frequently rode around our property and the neighboring fields until one day, I had another bad accident.

We were riding up a small hill about a mile from our house. Gray Man, with his longer legs, was faster than Curly. I yelled for Ed to slow down, but he didn't hear me. Curly, in his effort to catch up, became a bit unglued, and his canter was very unbalanced. I tried to slow him down, to collect his gait better, but he would have none of that, he had to catch up to his buddy. So he just bucked me off!

I don't remember flying through the air, just landing and not being able to breathe. I quickly remembered from my last bad fall that if I just yelled, my breath would come back and I'd be able to breathe.

As Curly galloped past Ed without me aboard, Ed immediately turned back to find me. My memories are hazy from then on. From what little I could remember, a stranger showed up in his truck on the old farm road almost immediately after I fell off. He said he saw a horse without a rider galloping across the road in front of him and his truck, and he turned into the trail, knowing something bad had happened. My cell phone was still attached to Curly's saddle, utterly useless. I don't like to think about how long it would have taken to be rescued if he hadn't noticed a rider-less horse running down the road.

Lying on the ground, I didn't feel the pain at first. I didn't lose consciousness, but I was in shock. I checked and could move my hands and feet, saying, "I can move! Nothing's broken! Owwwww!"

With the stranger's and Ed's help, I got into his truck. He drove me home, followed by Ed and Gray Man. I never learned his name, but I am eternally grateful to him. Another angel, or just a lucky coincidence?

The ambulance and paramedics soon arrived, and they decided to airlift me to the hospital. After determining that my spine was probably not broken, they carefully unloaded me from the truck to a stretcher, onto the helicopter, and off to the hospital.

The rest is a blur thanks to good pain meds. I spent the next three or four days in the trauma unit recovering from five broken ribs, a fractured shoulder (scapula), a punctured lung, and internal bleeding.

Allison, who joined us at the emergency room, told me it was difficult for the radiologist to determine what was broken, as I had multiple previous injuries from my first fall off a horse, a martial arts accident, and an ATV crash, all on the same upper right side of my chest. I was now up to twelve broken bones and two punctured lungs.

At home, I had the best of nursing care from Ed. Saint Ed. I recovered my health but not my love of riding. This was my second bad accident. The thought of riding filled me with anxiety and dread. A little PTSD? So I sold Curly, my beautiful palomino Tennessee walking horse.

It was difficult for me to admit that riding was not going to be the big, important part of my life in retirement that I had hoped and dreamed about. It was one of the few interests that Ed and I fully shared, and therefore I was not ready to give it up entirely. Instead, I bought another horse, Johnny, a little chestnut Rocky Mountain horse. He was barely above pony size, gentle and quiet. I had anxiety each time I got on him and said a Hail Mary at the beginning of each ride.

We again camped and rode the battlefields of Gettysburg and the beautiful trails of Acadia National Park in Maine, but riding was never quite the same.

Riding soon stopped being an issue the following year. Gray Man was bitten by a horse fly that summer. The bite never stopped oozing blood. A biopsy and then surgery confirmed a diagnosis of hemangiosarcoma, an aggressive form of cancer with a very poor prognosis.

We took GM home, and I sold Johnny. We borrowed an aging mare to keep GM happy and kept him until he passed.

Next "Job": Loudon County Medical Reserve Corps

⟍⟋

BUT IS THAT ALL THAT there is to retirement? If the meaning of retirement is just resigning from paid employment, what would give me meaning in life? I immediately got bored. Ed had plenty to do—finishing the barn and the house, landscaping, doing home maintenance and improvements. He started volunteering with Habitat for Humanity building houses. He was happy. Horses were great but not enough to fill my time and energy, especially now that we were not riding.

First I looked for a local chapter of the American Red Cross and was disappointed to learn that the nearby chapter in Leesburg was closed. I had been on the disaster mental health team in Vermont, assisting in local disasters such as ice storms, floods, and fires. I figured I could easily fit in here. Unfortunately, the nearest chapter was in Washington, DC, way too far.

Understanding me well, Allison came to the rescue. Working for the Loudoun County Health Department, she got me involved with the Loudoun County Medical Reserve Corps (MRC), which prepares for a variety of natural and manmade disasters, such as epidemics, terrorism, and weather catastrophes. It was similar to the volunteer work I had done for the Red Cross. No emergencies (yet), just annual immunization clinics, manning booths at county fairs and events, and teaching about Lyme disease and mosquito and tick control.

The MRC got more interesting once I joined its medical advisory board. Now we were preparing for weather disasters, bombings, terrorist attacks, anthrax, and a variety of plagues. I sat with eyes wide open with emergency workers, police, and firefighters learning how to spot terrorists and bombs hidden in packages. Unfortunately, nothing seemed impossible to me after 9/11.

With the horrifying occurrences of school shootings throughout the country, our county began to prepare. Cowering in closets and bathrooms, I was recruited to take part in active shooter drills, playing the role of victim as the police arrived and fired (blanks) at the "killers."

"You! Go to the boys' bathroom and hide in the stalls! You! Put this on" (an imitation bloody shirt) "and lie down on the bench. They are going to check on you, then take you out by stretcher. You! You are *dead*! Pick a place that looks clean and lie down." We were ordered by the police.

The bullets might have been blanks, but they were very loud! The police stormed the abandoned school we drilled in, and it was frighteningly real. Carted away on a stretcher, I thought of the reality of school shootings throughout our country. I had to take this picture of myself to make myself laugh. It was too grim.

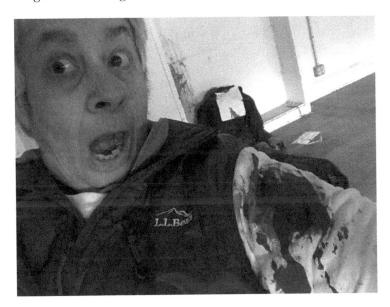

With no disasters thankfully in sight, I still had too much time on my hands. I read dozens of books, mostly novels, and joined two book clubs. I was a regular at the local library. Then I came across a book that changed everything. There it was among the other new books on the seven-day-only shelf of the library. I was up to date on all my favorite authors; adventure, spy, and detective novels were my specialty. I checked the best sellers in the nonfiction section and found *Proof of Heaven*. I glanced through the descriptions and noted it was written by a neurosurgeon at the University of Virginia who'd had a near-death experience. Hmmm. I took it home and read it in one day, then ordered five copies for myself from Amazon to give to my family. I had copies sent to Jason and my brother and sister, but I think I was the only person who read it.

It woke me from a twenty-five-plus-year spiritual sleep.

Here was an author with great credentials, writing about a multidimensional experience he'd had while in a coma. Remembering it all, he described a state of being that I had glimpses of while meditating decades before. I began meditating again, and it revived my interest in an old/new genre: the New Age. I dug out my old books on psi phenomena, reincarnation, and mysticism.

Second Hypnotic Regression

⌒

OUT OF CURIOSITY, AND THEN with a strong desire to find someone who specialized in hypnotic regressions, I compared researchers and schools of hypnosis. Finally, I chose the psychologist I thought would be the best for me. I wanted to learn about any past life I might have had and was curious about what I could experience in between lives.

I called for an appointment, and it felt like he was as eager to see me as I him.

"Hi," I said. "I was reading about Newton's hypnotherapy regressions and saw your name on his website. Do you have any openings?"

"Well, yes. You called at a good time. I just so happen to have an opening next week." Was I lucky or what?

I made the appointment and saw him in May 2013. I suspected that the market for regressions (with him) was slow, but I put this suspicion on the back shelf of my imaginary closet.

I drove four hours to get there and then spent another six hours in his office for the regression. I was particularly interested in what happens in between lifetimes. If one believes in reincarnation, then discovering the purpose for one's life *now* has meaning. I had already validated, with my experience in Israel, that I had lived before. Why was I here, in *this* lifetime, now? I longed to be connected to my spiritual guides and get any advice I could about my life purpose.

Well, I found this to be an expensive waste of time and money—$600 to be exact! I had chosen him as a therapist because he was a senior member of a particular style of hypnotic regressions. I had read about the theory and method of hypnotic induction used by his trainer, and, with my own experience using hypnosis, it looked like a good fit. However, Dr. A failed to use the standard induction as outlined in his mentor's book, and I began to have my doubts immediately. He also did not use the protocols advocated in the book.

When I finally did enter a past life, it was in a water world. I was a manatee/dolphin/mermaid thingy. How crazy! How could that be? There I was, under water, an aquatic mammal. Give me a break! I came out of trance and couldn't go back in. When I questioned him about this, he was defensive and blamed it on my failure to trust him, as well as my being a "hybrid soul." What the hell is that? Somehow I was not good enough? Huh?

It certainly was not what I had hoped for or expected. So much for hypnotic suggestion. I was so pissed I threw out the CD of the session he handed to me before I left in disgust.

That was a mistake. I would never have thought then, that my sub/unconscious/spiritual guides/higher self or whatever would want me to know this. Too bad. I thought the regression was a waste of time and money. However more weird events would prove me wrong.

Hospice and Reiki

I STILL NEEDED TO DO more with my time. Having worked full time for nearly fifty years in the helping professions, I hadn't adjusted yet to "retirement." What the hell is retirement anyway? Sitting on my couch, reading a book, watching TV, going for a walk with the dogs? Many might say, "Well, yes!" *Shpilkes!* That's the Yiddish word to describe ants in your pants, and that is exactly what I felt. I felt driven to do more. But what?

Now that I had researched near-death experiences, it seemed natural to me to explore dying. Not my own death, but what it means to others. My parents' deaths, and now my aunt Mimi's recent passing, made me more aware of getting older and what was ahead for me and Ed. That was scary. I hope I go quickly from whatever. Mimi had Alzheimer's for ten years before passing at age ninety-eight. Not a good way to go. Mom's death was faster, a heart attack and stroke before she reached eighty. Not bad. Dad's death, of cancer of the stomach in his late sixties, was long and painful.

So I did what I often do with my fears: I explored it. This spurred an interest in doing hospice work. I learned that hospice care is dedicated to assisting patients and their families within the last six months of life by offering comfort, not recovery. Medication for pain and nursing and spiritual care are provided by the hospice organization, with additional support by volunteers.

I first applied to a Washington, DC–based nonprofit hospice organization and waited for a response. And waited. I had filled out the lengthy application, signed a release for a background check, and supplied references. I wrote a letter asking if they had received my application. I called their office twice and left messages. No response at all. I guess they didn't need/want me.

When I told Allison about that, she immediately connected me to a friend of hers, another nurse practitioner, who had connections with Blue Ridge Hospice (BRH) in nearby Winchester. Lunching with Betsy Murphy, I discovered we had much in common beyond our nursing careers and interest in hospice care. Reincarnation, meditation, spiritual versus religious beliefs. Betsy and I both had memories of past lives and psychic/spiritual experiences. In addition to lunch, we spent a couple of hours eagerly comparing our lives, spiritual experiences, and paranormal experiences. The right person at the right time! She also gave BRH high marks for their health care and volunteer opportunities and encouraged me to apply there.

Betsy was right on. I was accepted immediately after applying, and I started volunteering as a respite caregiver at Blue Ridge, a nonprofit organization, after completing their volunteer training. Spending time with those who were dying, and with their families, giving support and lending an ear, filled some of the loss and connection I'd had with my clients at the Vet Center. I hadn't even known how much I missed it.

The purpose of hospice is to provide palliative care to patients in the last six months of life. I learned that means helping them be as comfortable as possible, as well as provide support for the family with in-home health care, emotional counseling, and spiritual counseling if desired. Having no fear myself of death or the afterlife, whatever that might be, made the care I gave very rewarding. As a volunteer, my time was a gift, and it was much more rewarding than I could have ever imagined it to be.

At first I just provided respite care. That meant relieving the patient's caregiver to give them time to do errands, keep appointments, and so on. I would sit and talk with my patients, hold their hand, offer liquids, read to them, or just watch them while they slept. Not much, but at least I felt useful to someone for a few hours a week. And very appreciated.

At the first hospice volunteer luncheon I attended, I met Kristin Zimet. I didn't know anyone there, but as I looked for a table to park myself, there she was looking at me. We introduced ourselves, and that was it! We were both from New York City and Jewish. The more we talked, the more it was evident that we were going to be friends. Beyond that, there was a deep recognition that we knew each other. She shared years later that she felt the same way about me.

I got to know Kristin and her interest in and practice as a Reiki master. I wondered how Reiki could provide healing to those in need. What did it do, and how did you do it?

I was still riding at that time, so I asked her about my horse, Johnny, who was resistant to being ridden. After I saddled him, he balked at walking into the riding ring. Despite her protestations, I pushed Kristin to come see Johnny and give him Reiki.

"But I never did Reiki with a horse before!"

"I don't care, Kristin. We need help!"

The first thing she did was scan him with her hand about six inches above his body. She started high on his neck, behind his ears, and slowly traveled down his neck, over his withers (shoulders), toward his spine. Johnny stood there quietly until her hand moved slowly over and above his withers, when he twitched dramatically. At the same time, I had an image of him from months ago, when he'd twisted and turned, then bolted during a storm. This was very vivid to me, as I was on his back at the time!

I now wanted to learn Reiki. So I did what I did best: I bugged Kristin until she finally agreed to teach me. As a plus, Mary Keith Ruffner, her good friend (and soon mine), and my friend Carol joined the class as well.

Carol Dennis was actually the first friend I met in Virginia. Stopping by my house after we moved in, she rang the doorbell and said, "Hi. I like your horse fencing. Can you tell me who built it?" That was all it took. Music, movies, and dinners with her and her good friend Jack followed.

I still find it difficult to describe Reiki after years of practice. Simply put, Reiki is a Japanese word that means spiritual energy. *Rei* means "spiritual," and *ki* means "energy," the same as *chi* in Chinese. I learned that this energy runs through everything in the universe, including plants, animals, and us. The Reiki practitioner channels this energy through her body and then to the patient, either using her hands directly on the body or by the patient's side without touching. She can even send Reiki to those at a distance for healing.

Reiki is a very personal transaction, practiced within a special, stylized format. I learned that in preparing to use/give Reiki, I start with a meditation and a prayer. I ask my spiritual guides for assistance and begin to feel an indescribable energy becoming available to me as it flows through my body from my crown, down through my spine. Peace and love envelop me. I can then send that to those who need it from a distance, or I can directly place it on my clients with my hands. Though I only touch them lightly, my hands become noticeably warm to both my client and me.

Who were these guides? I really had no firm idea. Were they angels? Jesus? Mary? Animal guides? A few years later, taking the Reiki master training, I had a beautiful merging with the Bodhisattva in meditation. We were as one, and I loved the thought of her guiding me.

I have learned to trust in the guidance of these energies to heal, support, and comfort those in pain and distress by observing it in action and getting feedback from my clients. Having witnessed the relief it gives to patients in the hospital as well as in hospice, I have no doubt about its efficacy for supportive care. It also reinforced my belief that in giving, we also receive.

I started doing Reiki by teaming up with Kristin at the Winchester Medical Center through their department of integrative medicine.

Every Wednesday, as volunteers, we went to the hospital and made the rounds of the medical and surgical units. I called it shopping for patients.

While walking through the hospital, we often encountered Wilbur, a beautiful and loving Goldendoodle. A therapy dog, he was always surrounded by nurses, visitors, and patients who adored this giving and patient animal. We couldn't pass him without stopping and giving/getting our love.

This reminded me of another story that Betsy told me about Sandy, a golden retriever who lived in the locked Alzheimer's unit of a local nursing home. Sandy brought love and peace to an often difficult patient population. Going home for breaks, she returned to her owner at night several times a week.

When we first checked with the nurses at the nursing station for those who might benefit, we were often greeted with, "Oh boy, I could use some Reiki myself." We made sure we had time to relieve the stress and strains of this valuable group of caregivers! Just ten minutes of Reiki in the quiet of the staff lounge was often enough to relieve headaches and relax muscles. We also gave Reiki to infants and mothers in the neonatal intensive care when requested.

I added Reiki to my hospice work. I felt like I was now able to do more to help my clients. It was a good fit, as I offered it for comfort and relaxation to both my patients and their families.

One of my favorite patients was Stanley. I first met him as he was sitting on his porch, one hand on his oxygen machine, the other smoking a cigarette. His house in the lovely Shenandoah Valley was surrounded by acres of farmland, trees, and hills. He was on hospice care for his COPD, chronic obstructive pulmonary disease. COPD disrupts the airflow in and out of the lungs and is most commonly caused by smoking. I introduced myself, and his sharp, immediate response was, "So, are you going to hypnotize me to stop smoking?"

"Uh, no," I replied. "Your nurse thought you might benefit from some Reiki." I then explained to him that Reiki might provide comfort and relaxation that in turn promote healing. If he stopped smoking, even better, but I wasn't going to hypnotize him. (Reiki masters never promote the practice as something that will cure illness, though occasionally healing occurs.)

"Okay, all right, I'll try it," he said grudgingly, and I assisted him to a lounge chair inside the house.

Initially resistant and doubtful, Stanley began to relax as I proceeded with Reiki by placing my hands on his head, then slowly down his body to his feet. Even before I got to his chest area, he was deeply asleep. Thus began a warm and trusting relationship we both enjoyed.

I did a home visit twice a week and gave Reiki to his mother as well. I can't even imagine how difficult it was for a mother to watch over her son as he was dying. I thought of Jason a lot at that time, so grateful he was well.

I continued visiting Stanley as his condition deteriorated, giving Reiki and providing companionship. Stanley talked about his fears about dying and came to accept the relief that death would bring as it became more and more difficult just to breathe. With encouragement, he talked about his beliefs in God and the afterlife, and together we laughed about reincarnation. I was careful to just listen and support him, without impressing upon him my own beliefs.

On Thanksgiving Day morning, at his request, I went over to his home and gave him Reiki for the last time. The next day, I was glad to hear that he was able to sit at the table with his family for the holiday dinner and later passed peacefully during the night. I received a beautiful thank-you note from his family, but I thank Stanley for his gift of sharing his last days and weeks with me.

Reiki is not a religion. It is practiced by those from a variety of religious traditions who wish to use this healing modality. Its basic message is one of compassion and selflessness. I deeply value the Reiki ideals, a prayer that I use daily, especially if I have difficulty falling asleep. (www.reiki.org)

Below is a poster of the Reiki ideals developed by its founder Usui Mikao, which I have on the wall over my Reiki table.

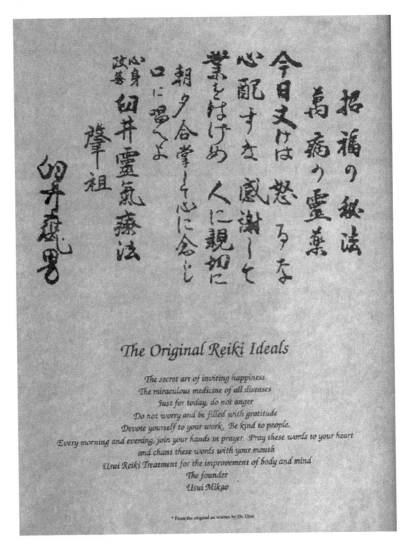

Animal Communication

In 2014, I watched a YouTube video of a woman named Anna Breytenbach "talking" with a rare black leopard named Diablo. Anna is an animal communicator in South Africa. She was visiting a rehabilitator of wild animals and was asked if she could help Diablo adjust to a new and better life at the center. He had been abused in a small zoo. He was so frightened he wouldn't leave his shelter in a small cage to explore his new and larger surroundings.

After communicating with Diablo, Anna was able to verify with his new caretakers many of the details of his former life, which totally amazed them. Now renamed Spirit, he was able to leave his nighttime enclosure and explore the much larger area for the first time.

I was very impressed, for two reasons. First, the black panther had been one of my favorite animals since childhood, and second, the idea of being able to communicate telepathically with animals was simply incredible! Could people really do that?

I did an immediate search for books on animal communication, devoured them, and then began to look for classes locally and for a friend to go with me. Carol jumped at the chance.

In short order, I began an animal communication practice group with just my good buddies Carol, Betsy, and Mary Keith, reading books and listening to the tapes. Kristin joined us when she could. We were in earnest and tried to meet weekly. Feeling the need for more information and practice, I found Janet Dobbs, a professional animal communicator, and Carol and I headed out to her next weekend class. Preparation for the class included reading J. Allen Boone's *Kinship With All Life* and Penelope Smith's book, *Animal Talk,* both fascinating to me.

The class was held on a beautiful farm. It was springtime, and the trees and flowers were in full bloom. The farm owner, who participated in the class, had a collection of horses, cows, chickens, dogs, and cats to admire, pet, and talk to. Six more eager women made up the class.

In the workshop we learned the basics of telepathy: first relaxing ourselves with meditation, then choosing an animal to practice on. With all the animals on the farm, and with pictures of each other's pets, there were no shortages of ones to choose. We had the owners of the pets for feedback, letting us know our hits and misses.

The highlight of the weekend for me was on the second day. We each were asked to choose a pet from the pictures we'd brought to class. The only information provided to us was the animal's age, sex, and whether it was neutered. Looking them over, I chose to do a reading on Helen's dog, Noble. I looked at the picture of a medium-sized, mixed-breed, three-year-old, neutered male dog. I relaxed and closed my eyes, picturing him. I then asked him if he would talk with me, and I saw him wag his tail as he agreed. For the first time, I felt a deep and unique connection with a nonhuman being. He was an intense dog, and he told me so much. When I say *he told me,* I don't mean in words. I didn't hear thoughts; there was just a knowing. I could feel his emotional strength and his love for Helen. He was also very anxious. I felt this as a tightness in my chest and my heart beating rapidly. I "saw" their white, two-story home with a white picket fence around the house and where he liked to dig in the yard. I felt him as a dog with high energy, pulling on the leash. He was hard to walk.

Noble shared with me his worries about Helen and how he wanted her to lighten up. He told me the other dog in the household had pain— from arthritis? He was also very suspicious of men, but he said Helen was lonely and needed a relationship. He then told me that she had been sexually abused and was afraid of men.

Too much info! I was anxious to tell Helen and the class what I had learned and see how much of it I was making up. If this was just my imagination, I was done with animal communication.

The pressure to share this was intense and I felt relief to talk about what I found out. To my great surprise, Helen confirmed it all: the white picket fence, the dog behaviors, the other dog's medical issues, and, especially relevant, the sexual abuse by a relative in childhood. I was stunned by the accuracy of what I had received from her dog.

Not all the exercises we did were that successful, but it convinced me that this was a very worthwhile endeavor to pursue. I resumed weekly practice with my group at home and then went to another, more advanced group taught by Janet a few months later. Back at the farm again, I did a detailed reading of one of the owner's horses that was quite accurate. I was beginning to feel more comfortable and confident in what I was learning and doing until Janet introduced a different exercise at the end of the first day.

On a table were several packages that she had gift wrapped. Our task was to choose one, then meditate on what was inside. After several minutes, I was finished. I drew a picture of the sun with a happy face. When I opened my box, I found a soup mix and cups decorated with farm animals. Wrong! So much for remote viewing. No one else's package contained my happy sun either. Now where did I get that image from?

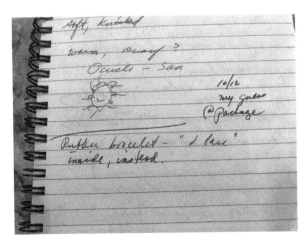

The next morning, when I arrived at class, there was a bracelet with a smiling metal sun on my chair. I was puzzled. It looked just like my drawing yesterday. Janet told me that the metal sun was what she had been *planning* on putting in a package but changed her mind! She thought I should have it. I now hang it on my bureau to remind me to trust myself more.

For our last exercise, we were instructed to walk around the farm and choose something to communicate with. Anything. A bird, horse, tree, rock, whatever. We all separated, and I wandered down a lovely path, wondering what to pick. How do you talk with something like a duck, bush, or stone?

Suddenly, I stopped in wonder before a huge, spreading tree with thick, convoluted branches reaching out in all directions. I had no idea what kind of tree it was (I later learned it was an Osage orange), but I was so impressed by it, I sat down on the ground and decided to try to communicate with it, not expecting anything to happen. To my surprise she welcomed me and told me, "I am the Grandmother Tree. Come. See me, and feel my roots growing deeply beneath you. I am old, 350 years old. I have been shattered by the elements, yet I continue to grow and thrive. Parts of me are dead and dying, while new sprouts and branches thrive."

"I give you my love and respect," I told her in awe.

"It is the same with you and your species. Some parts of your world are dying, yet some will survive. We will outlive your species if you all die. You have no respect for life or each other. It is very sad. We grieve for you."

"Do you have any advice for me?" I asked.

"Write the book. You don't have to save the planet. We will survive without you! Another will come, and the lessons will begin again.

"Yours is a learning planet—lessons must be learned over and over. Don't grieve. All souls will grow to God in their time. For some it may take many, many lifetimes and much pain. The outcome is certain. Let go of your fear and worry. Humans commit folly, painfully. *Write!* We will all help you. Look to the trees for wisdom."

It was so incredibly real! But I had no idea what she meant by my needing to write a book. This was 2014. What could I write about?

I was just beginning to put all these pieces together. Can thoughts really be discerned between humans, animals, trees and even plants by telepathy? Add in remote viewing, clairvoyance, clairsentience, angels coming to the rescue, and near-death experiences. How are they all connected?

Thankfully I have enough good friends to join with me in a monthly animal communication practice, to laugh, "talk" with our pets, and of course eat.

Poltergeist

I GASPED WHEN I SAW the photo: fourteen light bulbs, all busted in twenty-four hours. In that time, the bulbs, scattered throughout all three stories of the home, broke spontaneously, whether they were turned on or off. (Some of the broken bulbs are shown below in the photograph).

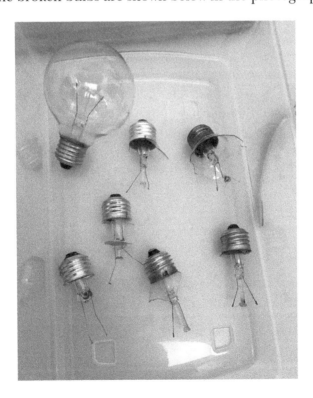

Allison called me that morning. The whole family, including Doug, her husband, and Luke, my twelve-year-old grandson, all suspected poltergeist activity.

They had never experienced anything like this before. They also called and got an electrician to inspect the wiring in the house and the fire department to check out the electrical feeds on the property.

"Mom, will you try to get rid of it with Reiki?" Alli asked.

"Okay!" I quickly agreed. Of course!

I went into the home and utilized the Reiki symbols and prayers in each room, starting in the basement. For good measure, I then sprinkled the holy water from Lourdes everywhere. Before doing this, I had called my friend Nancy Miquelon in New Mexico to have her ask her shaman friends what they do about paranormal activity. She asked them and they recommended I use "ghost brush" which grows wild alongside the roads in New Mexico.

The Apache tribesman use it to dispel any anger or negative emotions in the house. They light the brush and wait until the flame dies down, usually within a few moments, leaving it smoldering. They then go through the house and around each other. When it stops reigniting, the dark energy is gone. Worth a try! She immediately sent me a batch.

First I ignited it, then blew out the flames as directed, leaving just a slight smoldering. I went through the house, from the basement to the top floor. It did not reignite, which validated that what I had done before was successful. Poltergeist or whatever it was, was gone. And it never returned.

Dogfight

ED AND I WERE HAVING dinner at our neighbor Mary's house, surrounded by her four Norwegian elkhounds and three Russell terriers, all affectionate and friendly. Mary was a dedicated breeder and raiser of champion dogs, and we could always count on full laps while watching TV there. The seven of them would quickly cover us with love and hair. They were peaceful and calm in the house together, but I learned never to let them all out in the yard at once!

I already described the dogfight in the preface of this book. I still did not understand the full meaning of this. Then I had coffee with another friend, Leanne.

We were sitting down for coffee at the Firefly restaurant in Winchester,

Virginia. We greeted each other with big hugs, as we hadn't seen each other for a few months. Two busy women with full schedules. I had just given Reiki at the inpatient unit of our hospice center nearby.

I asked her what she was up to and listened avidly as she talked about her workshops and lectures. I admired her knowledge of the healing arts, Reiki, and shamanic practice. She was also a professional dog trainer.

I told her about my experience with the dog fight and asked her opinion. She then went on to describe an event she had had with her very well-trained German shepherd, Jackson.

"We were walking down the street when I noticed two dogs running toward us, growling fiercely. They were about a hundred yards away and coming fast. One was a rottweiler, the other a large mixed breed. I told Jackson to sit and stay and walked calmly and firmly toward the dogs as they approached, heads down, hackles bristling, teeth bared, and growling.

"Firmly, calmly, but loudly, I shouted, 'Stop!' and they did! I was not afraid. It was like I was in an altered state. I didn't feel anything but power and authority. It felt like it swelled within me from the ground up. The dogs stopped and ran back to where they came from. Jackson sat obediently and watched it all. He knew who was in charge!"

Leanne and I looked at each other. It felt so good to meet another person I could share this experience with, someone who not only understood it but had experienced it as well. The sisterhood was growing larger.

Virginia Master Naturalists

⌒

THANKS TO THE PRODDING OF Kristin and Mary K, Ed and I, as well as Carol and Jack, decided to take the Virginia Master Naturalist (VMN) training in 2015. The website states that "VMNs are volunteer educators, citizen scientists, and stewards helping Virginia conserve and manage natural resources and public lands." Just what Ed and I needed—a volunteer job/hobby that we could both do together, and with our friends!

The prerequisite was completion of a forty-hour seminar conducted over three months of training, done on Wednesday evenings and Saturdays, with lots of field exercises. We were taught basic concepts of climatology, ecology, geology, and other related sciences. In short, we were introduced to everything natural inhabiting our area from under the ground and up to the clouds, including a study of all the fauna and flora. I mean everything! Fish, worms, mammals, birds, trees, plants, and dirt. It was great!

Now that horseback riding was no longer a part of our interests, we found a new way to learn and spend our time together. We both had our separate interests, with Ed building houses for Habitat, and I had Reiki. Now we had something of importance and pleasure we could do together.

Monitoring bluebird boxes together in the spring is always rewarding and sometimes surprising. We never know what we are going to see—bluebirds, eggs,

or something else!

Within the first three years of moving south into "retirement," Ed and I had found meaningful volunteer work, wonderful friends, and a new and stronger relationship with our family. I felt so very blessed. I couldn't imagine anything else that would add to the meaning and quality of my life.

At the same time, I was reawakening spiritually. My spirituality had been dormant after the cult years, but now I was allowing myself to acknowledge that consciousness was much more than just my body, mind, and emotions. I could no longer deny that I was much more than my physical self.

The Grandmother Tree taught me this:

The wind whispers your name.
The rustling leaves brush against your feet as you walk your path.
The birds sing their songs to each other, and you rejoice in their voices.
The animals in and around your dwelling share their love for life with you if you pay attention.
Your brothers and sisters around the globe, around the universe, await your love and caring.
The earth is patient. She will be here forever, even if you are not,
Our souls are patient as well, watching you learn your lessons.

I had no idea that another mind-blowing adventure was just around the corner.

Part 6

Dulce and UFOs

"Breathe slowly, count back from twenty…Relax your head, your neck, your shoulders."

I watched in horror as my shoulders, then arms and hands, turned long, skinny, and bright green! Frightened, I came out of trance abruptly and shouted, "I'm turning into a praying mantis!" What the…

Dulce and the
UFO Highway

⌒

IT ALL BEGAN IN DULCE. Dulce, New Mexico. Every two years in November, there is an International Cultic Studies Association conference in Santa Fe. I was preparing to present a paper on treatment issues for recovering former members of cults. What better time to visit Nancy and Jeff Versaw, two old friends who lived in Dulce, then before the conference? Nancy, whose life in an Eastern cult has a chapter in my first book, *Captive Hearts/Captive Minds*, and Jeff both work as mental health clinicians for the Department of Indian Affairs on the Jicarilla Apache Reservation headquartered in Dulce.

This year we planned a trip to explore Chaco Canyon, return to Dulce for a few days afterward, then head to the conference in Santa Fe. A bigger agenda than I ever imagined!

Always the preparer, months before the trip, I first researched all I could about the mysterious, ancient Native American civilization at Chaco Canyon in northern New Mexico. Now a national park and a UNESCO World Heritage Center, Chaco had a relatively brief lifespan between (approximately) 800 and 1250 AD.

I first flew into Farmington, New Mexico, and was picked up at the airport by Nancy and Jeff. Both have a great sense of humor, and we laughed for a week traveling through the high desert atop the Colorado Plateau. Then on to Chaco Canyon. With its ancient ruins and kivas, it was mystifying and mesmerizing. Huge, it was used mainly, according to the Park Service guides, for ceremonial purposes, with people traveling hundreds if not thousands of miles from the south for religious ceremonies. Rumors of ritual sacrifice and cannibalism were whispered by various sources but unproven to date, adding to the Canyon's mystery.

I looked down into one of the giant kivas, a rock-lined circle perhaps one hundred feet in diameter that was open to the levels and rooms belowground. It was one of many kivas in Chaco, and I wondered about the ancient ceremonies held there both above and belowground, with various levels for rooms and storage. My imagination took me to the rumors of ritual murders and cannibalism.

When I asked one of the guides about it, I got a look of extreme annoyance, then denial. In any case, it was posited that a fifty-year drought had ended the civilization as all sources of water dried up. It was a reminder of the fragility of climate. Climate change, then and now, the destroyer of civilizations?

We then headed to Dulce before moving on to Santa Fe. I was prepared. Research had brought me to a book by Anthony Sanchez, *UFO*

Highway. I searched for it on Amazon and saw that it was listed but not available for purchase, new or used. Not one copy. Totally off the market. How could that be? It was listed but not available *anywhere*, at any price. Even my old book, *Captive Hearts/Captive Minds* which has been out of print since 1994, was available from book dealers on Amazon, often at a hefty price. I am glad I mentioned it to Luke, my then thirteen-year-old grandson.

"Here it is, Grandma!" He found a PDF copy on the internet for free, and I downloaded it. It had everything but the pictures.

I read it, fascinated by the account of a retired army colonel, kept anonymous for his safety, who chose to tell his story to Sanchez. He related that he was attached to a special medical unit, and his job was to assist in medical and psychiatric examinations and evaluations of military personnel under extraordinary and secret circumstances. Assigned to the military base underneath Archuleta Mesa for several years, he gave an extraordinary account of joint military research with extraterrestrials.

Archuleta Mesa overlooking the town of Dulce, New Mexico

The research, horrible as it was, included both abductions of people and mutilation of cattle. In interviews with the Jicarilla Apache tribesmen, Sanchez also recounts battles in the 1800s between the Apache and gray aliens. The Apaches lost and avoided the mesa. The various conspiracy theories were unbelievable but intriguing. Was this only science fiction?

This was my introduction to not only ufology but to alien abductions, hybridization of aliens and humans, and underground trains/rails between various military bases and Dulce. All for the joint alien/US research and development into military and civilian technology.

What brought Sanchez's informant to reveal all this was his inability to condone the experimentation on humans. As Sanchez recounts, his informant lives in total anonymity and in hiding, afraid of being found by the government as the source of information for the book. His reason for revealing the truth was simple: he stated he could not live with himself knowing what our government has done and continues to do in its dealings with extraterrestrials. Oh my!

Knowing about my fascination with the famed Archuleta Mesa, which loomed over the town, my friends arranged for us to have dinner with a couple of their Jicarilla Apache friends at the town's hotel/casino restaurant. Luzon, tall and lovely with a commanding presence, was one of the tribe's medicine women. She was reticent about talking to me. *About anything.* Strangers, especially white strangers, are not exactly welcomed on the tribal reservations. Considering Native Americans' history of murder and mistreatment by the US government, that is very understandable.

Nancy had told Luzon about my using the ghost brush to rid my daughter's home of poltergeists. I described what I did, how I first performed Reiki in each room, then tested my success by lighting the ghost brush. Since it didn't flame up, it seemed the Reiki had worked.

"Hmmpff," was all she said, staring hard at me as if looking through me. I don't think she wanted to believe that either there were poltergeists or that the Reiki worked.

Luzon was at first reluctant to talk about Archuleta Mesa other than to say she had explored it growing up. I pressed her, curious about her impressions. As a teen, she said, "My cousin and I were exploring, climbing the mesa, and we found some caves. We weren't afraid, so we entered the largest one. Then we heard the screams! Human screams coming from within, and we ran out as fast as we could. We didn't explore there much anymore!"

She said she was already familiar with the legends of alien and Apache battles in the past on the mesa. As for UFOs, she said, "We see them often in the skies above town, as well as the military helicopters. Cattle mutilations on ranches around the town are still ongoing." She asked me if I had seen the episode of History Channel's *Hangar One* series about the mesa. Unfortunately, I had missed that one!

The ICSA Conference in Santa Fe was almost anticlimactic after my adventures in Chaco and Dulce. I presented my paper on cognitive therapy to be included in ICSA's next book, *Cult Recovery: A Clinician's Guide,* and partied with old friends. But Dulce and extraterrestrials kept hanging out in the back of my mind.

MUFON: The Mutual UFO Network

⌒

I RETURNED HOME AND LOOKED up MUFON and found a chapter in Virginia. I went to that first meeting with my grandson. Luke was the only one in my family who would come with me. I think it was the hamburgers that appealed to him. It was interesting, and I started dragging whomever I could to the monthly meetings, or more often I went alone.

⌒

When Nancy told me there was going to be a UFO conference in May in Dulce, I immediately signed up and booked my flight. Looking up the speakers, I saw that Anthony Sanchez was going to be speaking about his book, and there were some other prominent presenters who were well known in the UFO community.

I ordered the book directly from his publisher, as it was no longer for sale anywhere else. When it failed to arrive, I called the printer.

"Hello. I ordered Anthony's book over a month ago, and it never came. What happened?" I asked.

"The post office returned it to us and said you refused it," she said.

"No! It never came!"

"Hmmm. That's happened to some other people who wanted the book too. I'll just send it to you again," she replied.

So she sent it again, and the same thing happened. The post office again said I refused it. I wondered if someone just didn't want me to have it.

"Anthony will bring you a copy at the conference," the printer said.

This gave immeasurable credence to what was in the book. If the government was restricting the market for it by making it totally unavailable through Amazon and its resellers, as well as *instructing* the US postal service to lie and say it was refused, then there must be something underneath that mesa.

As some people did receive the book from her, I wondered, Why me? Why didn't I receive it?

Dulce UFO Conference

I PICKED UP A T-SHIRT for my grandson, Luke, and couldn't wait to hear Anthony Sanchez speak about the secret government installation at Archuleta Mesa.

In addition to Sanchez, Linda Moulton Howe and Barbara Lamb were scheduled to speak. I of course ordered their books and read them ahead of time. These weren't as crazy or scary!

Howe's *Glimpses of Other Realities*, volumes 1 and 2, addressed crop circles, animal mutilations, extraterrestrial beings, and US military involvement. My brain was going click, click, click as past experiences and dreams from childhood onward were starting to come together, and maybe make some sense. I wondered if my angel appearing during the horse kick incident, my dreams of a council of monks, the scary figure at my bedside as a teen, and many others were maybe connected somehow.

Barbara Lamb's *Alien Experiences: 25 Cases of Close Encounter Never Before Revealed* was also fascinating and eye opening. As a practicing hypnotherapist, she regressed individuals who had seen UFOs and suspected they were taken.

I outdid myself. I arranged for a regression with Barbara before she left the Dulce conference and flew home. I also researched her background as a hypnotherapist, as my last regression was a disappointment. She was a good friend of Delores Cannon, who was a prolific writer about reincarnation and the purpose of life in the universe. I had already read many of her books and ordered the rest of them.

Sanchez was a disappointment. He appeared extremely anxious and did not say one word about his book or Archuleta Mesa, which loomed over the town. He avoided any questions about them or about why the book had been pulled from the market. He looked like he could use some Valium or a few stiff drinks. But I did finally get my signed copy of *UFO Highway*.

Howe's lecture was interesting, illuminating some of the highlights of her books.

Barbara Lamb's talk was about her new research and book, with Miguel Mendonca, called *Meet the Hybrids*. In it, eight people describe how they learned about being hybrids and how it affects their lives today. I hadn't read that one, and her talk blew my mind. Hybrids? Here I was, a newbie to the ocean of information on extraterrestrials, crop circles, animal mutilations, and oh, did I forget Bigfoot? I was on overload. I had already been told I was a "hybrid soul" a few years ago by the crazy hypnotherapist in 2012. Was this what he meant?

On the last day of the conference, in the morning in meditation, I asked my guides to help me understand the meaning of the experiences I have had all my life while in hypnosis and conferring with Barbara.

Another Regression

AT THE END OF THE conference on Sunday, I met Barbara in her room. She was rushed. We had barely an hour and a half before her flight. I wanted to know what a hybrid soul was from the previous regression. Did it have anything to do with the hybrids in her book? She said right off that there was no such thing as a hybrid soul. All souls, regardless of where they originate, are from the same source.

"A soul, whether incarnating as a human or an extraterrestrial, is the same. All souls are the same," she repeated. Hmmm. Confused, I asked her to explain this. The hybrids in her book, she said, had DNA from extraterrestrials added to their human DNA.

I was curious, not knowing what to think, so I lay down on the unused single bed in her room, knowing our time was short. "Okay", I asked. "Was I a hybrid? What is my purpose in life?"

"We will see." She replied.

"Now breathe slowly," she said. "Count back from twenty. Relax your head, your neck, your shoulders."

Obeying her suggestions, I watched in horror as my shoulders, then arms and hands, turned long, skinny, and bright green! Frightened, I sat up and shouted, "I'm turning into a praying mantis! I am *not* a Mantis!"

This brought me immediately out of the trance, midway through the induction. Barbara calmed me down, and with some difficulty, I went under again. This time I saw myself as a child embracing a tall Mantis, surrounded by love. However, I did not have any recall of any abduction, nor, with further exploration by Barbara, did I find evidence of being a human/ET hybrid.

She kept asking me while in trance to describe my eyes. I couldn't, because I was seeing *through* them, not looking *at* them. I *was* a Mantis, though only briefly. I didn't accept that until much later. In any case, she clarified that I was not an "abductee/experiencer." What was I then?

Again, I heard, my role is 'peacekeeper'. What does that mean? Sometimes I get answers that just don't make sense! But then neither do my questions.

MUFON and the Experiencer Research Team

~~~~~

RECOVERING FROM THE CONFERENCE, I returned home and couldn't wait for the next MUFON meeting. I was now even more open to the belief that the study of UFOs was rational and important. I wanted to learn more. I was also alone among my family and friends in this belief and interest. Saint Ed was supportive in my jumping off this cliff, as he always was in my pursuit of the weird and different. My family was used to this.

At the next meeting, I listened as one of the field investigators talked about his difficulty dealing with an individual who was deeply disturbed by an encounter with a UFO. It was hard for him to differentiate between her being hysterical or just upset, and he had difficulty doing his investigation of the sighting she had reported to MUFON.

This is it! I thought. This is how I can help! I raised my hand, introduced myself, and volunteered, as a mental health professional, to assist with any investigations where I might be useful.

His response was, "Great! Become a field investigator." So of course I did. What I didn't realize until I ordered the materials for the course was how involved and scientific the study of UFOs was.

The course is designed to teach the investigator how to rule out every other possibility so that the flying object is truly an unknown. That meant familiarizing oneself with various aircraft, weather phenomena, basic astronomy, and the use of tools such as altimeters, Geiger counters, and star finders. In addition, you needed to learn the resources in your area, such as local police, airports, and military installations, to confirm (or deny) unknown objects in the sky. And you learned how to categorize your findings in importance.

Another section of the course dealt with interviewing witnesses and analyzing photographic and other physical evidence. Eyewitnesses to contact with NHIBs (nonhuman intelligent beings) and abductions were another important area of concern, and they were of interest to me. Would I have the opportunity to interview and get to know them personally? I wondered how, and if, I could be of assistance to them.

The test was tough. Individuals are given three chances at passing, and I was very happy to pass the first time around. That was June 2016. In continuing to learn more about being a field investigator (FI), I ordered a DVD set of MUFON's investigator training series from the 2015 symposium. With that I hit gold!

The DVDs included a lecture by Kathleen Marden on abduction cases. In it, she mentions the need for more FIs to join the newly organized MUFON Experiencer Research Team (ERT) that she was heading up.

So, not one to let any moss grow under my feet, I immediately emailed her, filled out an application, got interviewed by her and two other members of the team, and voilà! I was now on the team. It was November 2016, exactly one year after my first trip to Dulce and five months after my first MUFON meeting.

I learned that the ERT has two main purposes. It was designed, with its experiencer questionnaires, to gather data from those who report contact and/or abduction experiences with NHIBs. But it has become much more than that. First, a person fills out the online questionnaire on the MUFON website, and then it is sent to a member of the team. (The Experiencer Questionnaire can be found in the appendix). As a team member, I then email the person a letter of support and offer to help them find resources in their area, such as therapists and/or support groups, as well as books and websites that may offer information. We also assist them in knowing that they are not alone and that research has shown that there are thousands of others who share their experience around the world.

To say that my view of the world has greatly enlarged since beginning work with MUFON and the ERT is a vast understatement. Of the hundreds of questionnaires that I have received so far, perhaps 60 percent have responded to my email invitation to correspond or talk with me. So whom have I talked to or exchanged emails with? They vary widely as to whether they are telling a narrative of their account, whether they have witnesses or proof in the form of pictures of their surroundings, NHIBs, orbs, or marks on their body, and whether they have memories that are based on hypnotic regressions or recalled without loss of consciousness. There are also many who have sighted a UFO and then lost time—minutes to hours—and who woke to find themselves dressed in bedclothes that were put on backward or with weird markings on their body and possible alien implants. Others, driving down the road when they spot a weird craft, find themselves miles down the road, far from where they last remember driving.

A variety of entities are also described. A very small percentage of the correspondents, less than 1 percent, have obvious mental health issues, are seeking attention without credibility, or are hoaxers. I googled one of my correspondents whose name triggered concern. He turned out to have a criminal record as a cyberstalker! I did not send him an email; instead I sent his name to the ERT research director, who put him on the "do not contact" list. That is a small list of fewer than a dozen people whom the team has concerns about for a variety of reasons.

When I joined the ERT, I found myself on a professional team that included medical doctors, psychologists/counselors, members of the clergy, journalists, scientists, and educators. All are trained as MUFON field investigators as well. From a handful of researchers on the team in 2015, it has grown, as of this publication, to over thirty-five volunteers in the United States, Canada, and Europe and receives about 1,400 questionnaires a year from around the world. The team is still growing! In addition to the experiencer questionnaires that are directly sent to the ERT, there are numerous cases of contact reported on the MUFON web-site, which are assigned to the individual's state directors, then us.

Almost half of the ERT team have also had contact with NHIBs and/or had paranormal experiences themselves. Do I include myself? Barbara Lamb, when I asked her after my regression, said I was not an Experiencer with a capital E, just an experiencer with a lowercase e. We laughed. I have never seen an extraterrestrial or been on a UFO or even seen one, *except in my dreams.*

Another Regression?

I WANTED TO KNOW MORE about *me*. I wondered if what I could recall now was all that there was to remember. So many of the experiencers regained memories with reputable hypnotherapists. I began to have a strong desire to try hypnosis again.

This time, I researched those who'd studied under Delores Cannon, a good friend of Barbara Lamb's who had died a couple of years ago. Delores Cannon's hypnotherapy, called quantum healing hypnosis technique (QHHT), seemed to fit in my trajectory. I found Patti Intorant, an advanced QHHT practitioner who lived a within a reasonable distance from me and made an appointment.

That day we reviewed my questions and interest in discovering past lives. Again, I wanted to know my purpose in *this* life, meet my spirit guides, and discover who I was in previous incarnations. In order to do this, I would be hypnotized, and with the guidance of my "higher self," we would review important past lives and be told my purpose in this life.

Patti and I spent the first two hours obtaining my history and planning what to explore, another hour or so in trance, and then over an hour discussing what I had learned. It was far from what I expected! What I saw in my trance is as follows:

> *Again, I find myself in a water world. I am under water, swimming peacefully and gloriously through the blue waters with what look like dolphins, blue whales or blobs, and manatee-like*

beings. All are very intelligent. What am I? Then I'm on another strange land/planet. It is red, dry, plain, and rather boring looking. I am building something with other indescribable, ant-like beings. Then I see a glowing city of light and more strange worlds and unknown beings. I ask, "What am I between lifetimes?" A Mantis!…Then, bliss.

I see myself. I am a shapeless being, ineffable, shining, iridescent, a rainbow of colors. When I ask what is my purpose in life, I am told again that I am a peacekeeper. Now what does that mean?

I came out of the trance confused. How could this be? I recalled little of what I had said under over ninety minutes of hypnosis, except the above. Even though we talked about it afterward, I recalled little more. I was happy to have Patti's recording of the session sent to me. But with her sound-dampening machine next to the recorder, I had difficulty listening to it. She immediately sent me her notes:

From Patti's notes:

After induction, I descend from "the cloud."

First past lifetime: I have no feet. I guess I am an energy body, just a vibrating energy form.

I find a tunnel and am traveling long and deep. Blue light. Underground way down. I see a huge pufferfish or sea urchin. I go around it. I am under water. I am swimming with fish. Blue whales or blobs. I have feet, three toes, and long legs that are spindly and skinny. I am an androgynous sea creature. Very intelligent!

Second past lifetime: Next I am floating in the sky above a planet or surface of something. Went from blue/pink to reddish and dark, another world. Bleak, dry, red, black. No structures. ??? I am a builder—creating places to live in like an ant. Group think. Easy life. Taken to end of life, and I am shedding a skin-like shell and leaving my body.

I am flying to a crystal city of light. I am floating around, looking for other energy sources. Then I feel warmth, bliss, surrounded by love. Oh, so wonderful to be loving oneness with the universe, no separation of self from the universe!

Next Patti had me separate myself from my oversoul? Big Mady, not little Mady, me.

Big Mady said, "She's not of the Earth. She/I made the Earth! We are a Mantis being. The water world is a vacation place to rest, play, and have fun.

"Her role(s) are in the transition—working to create the new Earth. She will be teaching, helping souls of transition to ascension. Spiritually.

"After this lifetime she will be a spiritual guide. Her role in this one is one of leadership—keeping peace, a balance of the light and dark. Peacekeeper (again!).

"She has no karma needs. Her weight has the task to anchor her in humanity. She chose that.

"She needs to be reminded that she is the universe. She must remember she is the creator.

"She has been a warrior for the Source. There have been worlds at war, forces that are destructive.

"She has no fear. She defeats negativity with love.

"Advice for Little Mady: (1) She needs to remember who she is and reunite herself with the Source. Instead of asking for help, she needs to remember that she is the help she asks for. Remember to be one with them; she is not separate from them. And (2) Purpose of cult experience was to learn about evil/dark nature of some humans."

It was difficult for me to comprehend all of what I heard in the recording and read in the notes Patti sent to me. Did I really say those things? What was clear was that I *did* have many extraterrestrial lifetimes, and it validated my previous regression four years before, when I was also in a water world, though I refused to believe it then. I was stunned.

Now I also longed to return to those many worlds, to see and experience them more. I missed them. I also wanted to understand what being that "ball of fire" meant. My essence? What is that? Where to next? What is this Mantis thing? How do I get there?

I could not understand and accept the full meaning of that regression. That would take more time and study. And more adventures.

One more question: What is a higher self or oversoul, and did I really contact that part of myself?

.

Into the Stars

$\longrightarrow$

I WENT ONLINE AND LOOKED up Cynthia Crawford, whose story is told in Barbara Lamb's *Meet the Hybrids*. Cynthia has sculpted a myriad of the extraterrestrials she encountered during her amazing life. I hoped that she could identify what I had recalled in my regressions. At thirty-four, she found out she was a hybrid when her father, while a medical doctor serving in the military, told her about the experiments that were done to create new beings with superhuman functions. Her mother was one of those chosen to have the DNA of extraterrestrials added to Cynthia while she was still in the womb.

Looking at her website, www.etsculptors.com, I saw several of her sculptures of dozens of extraterrestrials. I was amazed, not by seeing the commonly known "grays," but at the others—Andromedans, Sirians, Pleidians, and more. Then I saw the Nebulan Healers. They took my breath away! That's who I had seen at my bedside when I was thirteen! Her website explained that "they protect those who are helping others necessary to the higher evolution of mankind. Cloaked, with head coverings only exposing their eyes, they are watchers and helpers for mankind." I immediately felt relief with this explanation of an episode in my life that had previously only brought fear.

I called Cynthia, and we had a long talk. Even over the phone, I could tell she was a wise and loving person. I wished I had known her long ago. She was also very psychic. When I described what had happened to me years ago, she validated that it was a Nebulan Healer, and she told me stories of many other healings that they had done, including one on *her* that inspired that sculpture.

I told her that I wished to buy one of her sculptures but didn't know which one. She suggested I download pictures of those that appealed to me and meditate on the one that drew me the most. I ordered an Andromedan. The Mantis being was too cute and didn't represent those I saw in meditation and regressions.

I got to know Cynthia more in further telephone conversations. She was always welcoming, loving, and encouraging. I am sorry I missed her at one of the few conferences we both attended before her death from cancer. Now I have four of her imaginative sculptures, including a Mantis she made for me.

Before she died, she recommended that I contact Jacquelin Smith, another hybrid that Barbara Lamb wrote about in her book, for a star origin reading to determine whether I was of Mantis origin. So I did.

Jacquelin Smith

I FIRST BECAME FAMILIAR WITH the work of Jacquelin Smith from a couple of different sources. As a well-known animal communicator, she produced both DVDs and books on communicating with our fur babies, some of which I had already purchased a few years before. Her story was also recounted in Barbara Lamb's book *Meet the Hybrids.*

In checking out her website, I saw that she did star origin readings. Highly psychic, she would do a reading and let you know the "origin," meaning the first expression, of your soul. This is not to say there is a difference in people's souls but in their *first* expression, or what she calls your core "soul self."

I told her about my regression with Barbara the year before and my questions about the Mantis. Her immediate response was, "That doesn't mean your origin is Mantis." I took this to mean she doubted it.

Upon meditating and asking her guides, her response was, "Yes! The Rainbow Mantis is your soul family." She then taught me a simple mantra to connect with them as a group and another to directly connect me with my higher self, the particular Mantis that I originated from.

She encouraged me to meditate on my higher self for support, love, and assistance in resolving questions, following my path, and getting help in just about anything.

Doubtful, I began to do just that. But she was right. More on this later.

"What is the Rainbow Mantis? How do they differ from other Mantis beings?" I asked Jacquelin to tell me more about them, who they are, and what purpose they have in the universe. Several months later, she wrote the following to me about Mantis beings. I've reprinted it with her permission.

"I always enjoy communicating with Mantises. They are highly intelligent and also express a wide variety of emotions. When I see a Mantis ethereally and quasiphysically, they are about eight or nine feet tall, but they can range in height. They look similar to a praying mantis, but they do not have claws on their upper appendages. I love looking into their beautiful, large black eyes. They have with a triangular face. Also, they appear to have six appendages like a praying mantis. They are upright. There are various species and subspecies of Mantis who appear to me as different colors, which is their frequency. They also have third-eye lasers, which are used for various tasks.

Part of the role of Mantis beings is to bring about order from chaos. Mantises assist with the evolutionary process. This includes assisting with other beings and worlds. They are true cocreators. Mantises have the ability to create star systems, worlds, and other beings. They set up the grids energetically for other star systems and worlds. Also, Mantises assisted with creating grids for Earth. They simply set their intention in order to create.

Mantises are masters of genetic codes and at creating holographic energy bodies that then can manifest into forms or a quasiphysical manifestation or expression. This is a big part of their work. They also help with integrating timelines.

They work in cooperation with other beings in doing all of this work. Some of the other beings are of the celestial realm, as well as dolphin-like beings and those of the elemental realms, including fairies, gnomes, and many others.

They help set the planets, stars, and star systems into motion and then step back to let them evolve on their own. They can erase other star systems, worlds, and beings that they have created. This is all part of the creative process and is done from a sense of creative play. Also, Mantises are excellent at transmuting and balancing what we would think of dark and light.

Mantises are an ancient race, and even though they are highly evolved, they, along with every living being, are continuing to evolve. They help create and watch over the cosmic grids.

The Mantis races care deeply about Earth and are here to assist humanity in their evolutionary process. There are many people on Earth who have connections with the Mantis races and who have Mantis frequency in their star DNA. I have a high percentage of Mantis in my star DNA, so it's natural for me to connect with Mantises.

I've been communicating with at least eight different races of Mantis. I refer to them as colors. I can see the colors or frequencies of who they are. For example, there are black, white, pink, golden-tan, neon blue/purple/green, rainbow, and many others. Each carries its own frequency/color. When I communicate with them, I can feel and see the differences. I find all of them kind, loving, and gentle.

In general, Mantises are very gifted at being able to understand the bigger picture of the cosmos and beyond. At the same time, they are good with details in their work. They are highly evolved in this way. And yet Mantises are playful and love to have fun, laugh, and dance. They are childlike but not childish. They have a great sense of humor as well.

All Mantises I have met have wonderful healing abilities. They have a laser in their third eye that they can use for various kinds of healing. Also, they perform healing work by transmitting their frequencies through someone's physical and etheric bodies. One time, eight Mantises were standing around my bed when I woke up. They wanted to dance with me. I complained, "It's too cold. I don't want to get up." They kept asking me to get up, like five-year-old children would do. So I got up, and we danced together. Suddenly, my neck snapped, and they aligned my spinal column. It was a surprise! Mantises also offer healing with emotions as well as the soul.

They are excellent with holographic healing. They can shift energies within a person's holographic body so that they can heal. Also, Mantis beings can activate light codes by just being present interdimensionally. Mantises have given me many light codes. I draw them on paper, and this also activates people. Also, when I speak the light language of Mantises, this activates people and whatever other life forms that might be around.

I have always had fun and have had amazing experiences with Mantises. They are always willing to assist if we ask them. The healing they perform may come in ways we don't always recognize or understand. This is because they are doing their work from a higher plane and frequency and can see the whole of things better than we can.

Mantises make me laugh and are heart centered. I always feel joyful when they come to visit me. They wanted me to share this with you: "We serve divine love. We care about Earth and all species on Earth. We come with open hearts."

Wow! Could that be true? But then, I have loved Mantis' since childhood. A coincidence?

I find the above almost unbelievable. How do I make this stuff up? Am I left with the choice of believing this is all crazy and accepting only the concrete world I observe through my five senses? Or do I reach out with my heart and embrace what comes to me in my dreams, meditations, and yes, regressions?

I choose the latter. I have been blessed with a wonderful life. Though I am not by any means wealthy, all my material needs are met. I have a loving family and some very dear friends who share many of my views on life. I suffer nothing. But there is suffering all around me.

Elizabeth Kolbert writes, in fascinating and horrifying detail, about the threat of a new era, aided and abetted by mankind, in *The Sixth Extinction*. Climate change, loss of species, famine, droughts, and warfare cannot leave me smug in my contentment. Daily, the media bring awful news of the struggles of untold millions of our fellow human beings.

I look for meaning in life. Is it just to be here for a few decades to survive and entertain ourselves, to buy things? Is happiness sought by buying more, bigger, newer, better? How can that be when millions of people struggle for food, medical care, and even water?

Yes, I can improve some things. I can help others with Reiki and by giving support to those dying, doing hospice work; preparing for disasters, natural or manmade, with our local medical reserve corps; and of course being part of MUFON's ERT. In doing so I seek ways to awaken further to the truly meaningful aspects of existence.

Debra's Story

⌣⟶

My journey through life echoes with those who I have helped, particularly those experiencers who have wondered some of the same things as I. Not too long after I joined the ERT, I was referred to Debra.

The following account first appeared in a chapter I wrote for Kathleen Marden's book, *Extraterrestrial Contact: What to Do When You've Been Abducted*. It is reprinted with permission.

Debra filled out our experiencer questionnaire and responded to my invitation for a call. In her initial email to me she wrote, "It happened about twenty-two years ago, but it was like it happened yesterday. I was pregnant with my daughter, I would say only a few months, when I went to take a nap. In the middle of my sleep, suddenly, my body was being sucked up into a tunnel as like a tornado, but with a very loud, ear-piercing sound like a hum. The sucked-up feeling was like a whirlwind. All I could do was call my son's name. I didn't know the reason for my calling him, but I knew I couldn't leave. I had to return to my son.

"The next thing I knew, I was on a table covered in white sheets. It looked almost like a hospital room. It had stainless-steel cabinets on the wall [and a] stainless-steel table, which I was lying on. My body was covered and my eyes were closed, yet I saw everything—even heard them talking—but couldn't make out what was being said. I communicated with them telepathically, and all I could say was, 'I have to go back. My son needs me.'

"There were several beings around my table on all sides. They were wearing brown robes, but I could not see their faces. They were wearing hoods. The robes had belts with tassels on the ends. The sleeves were long, as were their robes, with angel arms, almost like a bell-bottom sleeve.

"They were now communicating with me telepathically, but I at this moment heard them in English. In the upper left-hand corner, over my shoulder, was a being that was near a curtain, which was very long. He lifted his arm up and caught the curtain in a sweeping motion with his arm. As the being swept the curtain back, there was a light that was so intense I had to squint my eyes. The being then asked if I wanted to go to the light or come back. I yelled again, 'I have to go back to my son! He needs me!' BOOM! I was back in my body so hard my whole body almost jumped off the bed.

"I was terrified of what took place, so scared I made an appointment with a cardiologist to see if I'd had a heart attack or died. He took a few tests and told me no.

"Since then I have awakened many times, thinking, 'Are they still coming for me?' I don't have a clue. But almost nightly I think about that terrifying time and hope it never happens again."

Coincidentally (or perhaps not coincidentally), I was the ERT member to receive her questionnaire and invited her to correspond. I had also had an experience with a tall, brown-robed and hooded "creature" when I was thirteen years old. I could not see its face, as the cowl of robe covered its head. In looking back, I thought it was the Angel of Death or the Grim Reaper without a scythe. I remember having some sort of respiratory infection at the time. I screamed for my mother, and it disappeared. I learned what "it" was during a conversation with Cynthia Crawford, another experiencer, who sculped various extraterrestrials from around the universe. I had been looking for one for my Reiki room, and she directed me to her website at www.etsculptors.com. I looked at the artwork on her website and was shocked to see the photo of the same robed being that I now know as a Nebulan Healer. The Nebulan Healers, according to her website, work with the Galactic Federation, protecting (certain) individuals to ensure their survival for roles in the future.

Without disclosing my own experience, I directed Debra to the website and asked if any of the sculptures resembled the beings she saw. Excitedly she picked out the Nebulan Healers as those she saw, but she said she was not ill when abducted. She then said that though she was not sick, her obstetrician had told her, after multiple tests, that her unborn child [had] Down syndrome, and he urged her to have an abortion. She refused. However, a few months after the abduction, her child was born normal! Originally terrified of the memory, she now feels blessed by the experience. This example illustrates again how important support, confirmation, and information is to "normalize" extraordinary experiences.

Why is this so important? Here is only one example of two individuals, the experiencer and the ERT member, separated by thousands of miles and several decades, sharing a healing experience by similar entities. Both of them were initially terrified by them due to lack of understanding.

Working with Debra and hundreds of others who have had contact experiences as well as abductions has been healing for me as well as them. In helping them, I too come to terms with extraordinary events that would otherwise tend to isolate me.

This is a photo of (from left to right) Ann Castle, me, Kathleen Marden, and Denise Stoner. We all contributed to Kathleen Marden's book, Extraterrestrial Contact: What to do When You Have Been Abducted. We had a *lot* of fun and best of all, became good friends.

Kids and UFOs

WHAT DO YOU TELL CHILDREN, I mean *little* kids, about UFOs and extraterrestrials? It never occurred to me to even think about this until I got asked.

Ella contacted MUFON for info on UFOs and contact with extraterrestrials, because her favorite after-school group wanted information. They had just studied cryptozoology and Sasquatch and now wanted to know about aliens. We supplied her with a lot of information about different types of UFOs and how field investigators differentiate them from aircraft, balloons, satellites, stars, and so on—in other words, what makes them *unknown or unidentified.*

Ella described her after-school, extracurricular class of about twenty-five very bright kids who wanted to learn more about this and other worlds. They wanted to know if UFOs are real. Does life exist outside our planet? What is MUFON? What do I do? And a gazillion other questions, all of them good!

This brought up some problems and issues. First, many of the people who answer MUFON's ERT questionnaire are frightened of their experience until they get support or counseling and referrals to support groups or hypnotherapists. We quickly agreed to leave out the entire subject of abductions aboard spacecraft. But I wanted to include in our talk nonfrightening information that we have gleaned from those who have been in contact with nonhuman intelligent beings.

Several calls and emails later, I agreed on a date to come and talk with her and her class. In the meantime, they put together a list of questions for me to address, and Ella emailed them to me. Thus prepared, I headed out for the town, an hour away from home, wondering what to expect.

Ella greeted me warmly and ushered me through the maze of hallways to the classroom. I looked in and saw about twenty-five little kids! What was I doing here? Aged seven to eleven, they may have been young, but I quickly realized they were very bright and surprisingly sophisticated for their age. And they were prepared for me. After the introduction, I began with their questions. I started by explaining that I didn't have all the answers but would do the best I could. Each question began a discussion. These were their top ten:

1. What do you think an alien looks like?
2. What was your weirdest case?
3. Have you ever seen an alien spaceship?
4. What was one of the creepiest cases you ever had?
5. If you could describe aliens in one word, what would it be?
6. What was your favorite case?
7. How long have you worked for MUFON?
8. How many fake calls have you received? Please tell us the story.
9. Have you ever seen an alien in real life?
10. When and why did MUFON start?

I only had forty-five minutes to answer all those questions, and these children were very sophisticated, piling on even more questions as I talked. It was a challenge. I wanted to be very careful and not frighten but enlighten them.

What fun they were! I began by defining "alien," telling them that alien simply meant something foreign or unknown and was a commonly used word to describe something strange, something we don't know about and are possibly afraid of, such as "illegal aliens." I added that, to extraterrestrials (my preferred term), we are the aliens!

From there, I asked them, "Do you ever feel different than other kids? Uniquely different?" They all nodded their heads in agreement.

I showed them Cynthia Crawford's sculptures of aliens on her website, www.etsculptors.com. Each were different, I said, and all were benevolent. I stressed throughout the talk that all the ETs we were discussing were being very helpful to humanity and looking out for our best interests. I admitted that possibly some were not so good, but I didn't have knowledge about them.

As my favorite cases involved healing of physical problems and health issues, I talked about my own healing from illness as a thirteen-year-old, showed the NHIB (with picture) that healed me, and described the many cases of healing among the experiencers I'd worked with in the past two years. I showed them the new 785-page book from FREE (The Dr. Edgar Mitchell Foundation for Research into Extraterrestrial and Extraordinary Encounters), *Beyond UFOs: The Science of Consciousness and Contact with Non-Human Intelligence*, which dedicated a chapter to healings by ETs.

As for fake cases, I had to admit that it was sometimes hard to tell, though some were obvious from the names they used to describe themselves or the information they provided. In my two years on the team, I could only be sure of two fakes. One of them turned out to be an internet stalker. I didn't tell them about him!

I responded only indirectly about the weirdest and creepiest cases. Aren't they all weird and creepy by their very nature? They agreed that the unknown was scary. There is a ready market for those stories, true or false, on TV, in the movies, on the internet, and in books.

The only easy questions were about MUFON—why it started and so forth. Nuts and bolts. Easy.

I came away from that talk impressed by the seriousness and interest among young people on this very esoteric subject. They took cryptozoology seriously and now were doing the same with life outside of our world. I felt hopeful after talking with this group. They were more open than some of the adults I encounter daily.

A Few Words of Advice

MY PATH HAS BEEN LONG and winding, with many ups and downs, trips and falls. I thank you for traveling it with me. Many of those I have consulted with through MUFON's ERT are puzzled by the numerous and unexplainable events in their lives. Sorting through the huge amount of information and yes, misinformation available through the media about psychic phenomena, consciousness and ufology is a tremendous task. I have some suggestions:

In order to make sense of my own history, I chose first to write it down. Only you can sort through and find meaning in your life.

1. Start simply with a timeline of events. When you have time and feel inspired, describe those events.
2. Keep a journal about your thoughts, feelings and dreams. Write down all the experiences that perplex, excite and confuse you. Their meaning may become clearer to you over time as you look at them in sequence.
3. Be careful who you go to for advice. The New Age gurus of the '70s and '80s have reproduced like rabbits. Through television, the internet, books and even games, we are constantly exposed to those who would profit from our search for the truth. Robert Cialdini's book, *Influence* is an excellent source of information to help you sort out who is likely to be helpful or harmful. I strongly recommend it!

Through much of my life I would have described myself as trusting, if not gullible. Always hopeful, I looked for the best in others and sometimes found the worst. I bought lots of lottery tickets!

You have read about my contacts and resources in this book. As much as I have been delighted and surprised at some of the information that I have learned from others about myself, I take it all as an often entertaining, if not truthful account of my being. Maybe yes, maybe no. Does it enhance my life and give me the strength and encouragement to be the person I would like it to be? Or did it alarm me, like the tarot reader in **Part 1** who foretold (falsely) a pregnancy and abortion? Did I end up turning over my life and savings to a sociopathic social worker? Yes (sigh).

I have encountered individuals who promised 100% accuracy of their psychic readings and predictions. Others guaranteed that you would have ufo encounters. These promises may be costly, time consuming and wasteful. I find that alarming. Please use some due diligence in investigating their claims. If it sounds too good to be true, it probably is. You be the judge. Google them, check it out! Get the opinion of others in the field. The more unusual the offer, the more evidence you need to discern the truth.

In addition, do you have any niggling thoughts or doubts? What are the pros and cons? Perhaps most important of all, honor your gut.

What's Next?

WITH A FIRM BELIEF THAT we not alone in this universe/multiverse, I am now wondering what my next steps in exploration are.

Meditation and even hypnosis have been my ways of seeking knowledge of and supporting my belief in a continuation of life beyond this dense plane and planet. I believe that my soul and all souls are one, a part of creation, a part of God/Gaia/the Creator/the Source/All That Is. That there is purpose in life, that we are *together* growing in knowledge of ourselves and our connection to each other, here and in the universe.

Meditation and calling upon my higher self for guidance for both mundane and profound issues has become a part of my daily routine and has led the way to this book.

Simply put, I am certain that I am much more than my body. That consciousness is cosmic and that we are all one, including those intelligences throughout the cosmos and other dimensions.

With this in mind, I enrolled in courses at the Monroe Institute, whose beliefs I found echoed mine. I am convinced there is no end to discovery and the journey never ends.

In meeting Frank DeMarco, who participated in research with Bob Monroe, I quote here from his book *Muddy Tracks* (pp. 341-345) what he learned at the Monroe Institute:

He believes, and I concur:

1. *We are immortal spirits temporarily inhabiting bodies.* Our spirits form, maintain, and live in our body, but we are much more than that.
2. *This life is not our only life.* We existed before this physical lifetime and will continue to exist after our body passes.
3. *We "individuals" are all connected to one another.* We seem to think that our bodies are what separate us from one another, but the newest research in physics acknowledges the interconnectedness of all in the universe.
4. *We as individuals are fragments of a larger being that cares about us and can be trusted.* Call this our higher self, God, the universe. Over the years, in meditation, I have come to trust this connection and feel its support and love.
5. *Nonetheless, this larger being sees things differently.* It is not bound by our 3D world and does not forget its or our purpose in this material world.
6. *The larger being is a source of foresight and wisdom.* It cannot direct our lives for us, as our choices, both those that are seemingly harmful and wrong as well as those that are inspired, all direct our growth, which is the purpose of incarnation.
7. *The larger being contacts us, sometimes sending dreams, sometimes hunches or "knowings" or precognitive flashes...And this is not a one-way street.*
8. *We can contact the larger being.* Through prayer, meditation, and asking for guidance, we have access to our higher selves and its wisdom and guidance. They are there for the asking!
9. *Thus, our lives need not be disconnected and solitary.* I like DeMarco's comparison of the individual as a finger of a much larger hand. The fingers are not separate from each other. We are never alone, though it certainly may feel that way at times.
10. *Nonetheless, we may often lose communication.* This connection cannot be severed, but it can be forgotten, distorted, and neglected. Many have never learned it exists and therefore have yet to discover it.

If You Got Lost

If you got lost I would find you
If you got hurt I would help you
If you got trapped I would save you
If you got abducted by aliens
I would cripple their ship's computer system
By uploading a virus somehow
For you I would swim across the deepest ocean
For you I would jump across the widest chasm
For you I would race across the largest country
So now that you know
All that I would gladly do for you
Maybe you could do something for me
And give me a braver name than "Wiggles"?
—Francesco Marciuliano, *I Could Chew on This: And Other Poems by Dogs*

Lilly and Scooter, my two precious corgis.

Conclusion

Is there ever a conclusion? Can one ever state that they know now all there is to know about anything, even everything about oneself? I am glad I don't have the hubris to tell you or anybody that I understand or even believe in the veracity of all I have experienced.

I do have a word of caution: I am not cemented to the absolute truth of all I have experienced. I take it all with multiple grains of salt! Proof? I have no proof. I have only used my experiences and memories to help others and myself navigate the convoluted path of life.

From childhood to the present, my dreams, the events in my life, the meditations and hypnotic regressions have all revealed an unlimited consciousness that I can accept or reject. What I do choose to believe is that we are all equally a part of God our creator. That means that *all* our souls, regardless of when we begin our incarnations, on whatever planet or realm we start our growth, are of the same material. None is any better (or worse) than any other. What we do with our lives, in *this* lifetime is the only thing of importance.

What we each do with that gift of life is something different for everyone. I have experienced personal encounters with humans that some would call evil. I watch the political climate as well as our earthly climate and wonder how others can deny or ignore critical areas that need change now (or better, yesterday). I believe our future on this planet is in danger due to our willful neglect and destructive and greedy plundering of resources.

In this book I have recounted many wonderful, powerful, and often puzzling events in my life. I cannot prove or disprove anything. That is not my job. I can only be a witness to the world I observe, to the events within and around me. Personal growth cannot occur without challenge and without a change in our consciousness toward a loving benevolence for all life.

My wish for all is a growing awareness of what is important in life, of the fact that love for ourselves and compassion for others are gifts from our creator. With that love, all beings, including animal, mineral, and extraterrestrial, are equal and deserving of our care.

Acknowledgments

Because this is a book about my spiritual journey, there were many stops along the way, as well as hurdles. The hurdles, I now know, were not so much impediments as kicks in the butt to my growth. They just didn't feel like that at the time!

First of all, I have been blessed with a wonderful husband, Ed, and family, Jason, Allison, Luke, and Doug. They may not have known the strange directions I was going to wander, but they stayed by my side with love and support.

I am deeply grateful for the many wonderful people who supported me on this journey. I would like to thank:

My very special women's circle: Carol Dennis, Kristin Zimet, Betsy Murphy, Mary Keith Ruffner, Joanne Hart, Margaret Wester, Leanne Kamber, Lorraine (Quiche) Nordland, and Elizabeth Bava, who explored with me animal communication, Reiki, hospice care, and more.

Joseph Mancini Jr. and another "circle" for their support and encouragement.

MUFON and beyond: Kathleen Marden, Ann Castle, Denise Stoner, Teresa Tindal, and all on the Experiencer Research Team. Jacquelin Smith and the late Cynthia Crawford for their extraordinary expertise and guidance.

Oh, the cult days! Joe Kelly, Pat Ryan, the late Kevin Garvey; Carol Giambalvo and her beloved, now deceased husband, Noel; Hana and Jerry Whitfield; Michael Langone; Lorna and Bill Goldberg; Roseanne Henry; and Nancy Miquelon: all supportive, caring, and knowledgeable friends.

Thank you, Laura Chernow! What a wonderful kick-start you gave to me with the book! I have tried to follow your example throughout.

At the Vet Center, a big thank you to Dick Chase, Larry Caruso, Terri Munsey-Ballou and Leon Blackmon whose stories I shared in this book. And thanks to *all* the veterans who bravely served our country and who allowed me to travel with them through their battles and traumas as we healed together. You were all my favorites!

I must also include my furry/feathered friends past and present, as they inspired me with their love and companionship: Chickadee, Simon Bird, Samson/Delilah, Tojo, Sonya, Tobi, Tara, Jessie, Squeakman, Yogi Bearski, Indy, Lucky, Scooter, and Lilly. Numerous kitties since childhood, Frosty, Ben and Jerry, and Freddie. Horses I have known and loved: Maya, Tiki, Babe, Gray Man, Curly, and Jonnie.

And of course, all the blessed animals at the Bronx Zoo!

Appendix

The Experiencer Research Team
MUFON Experiencer Questionnaire
Do you agree to be contacted?
Provide your name, email address, city, and state.

1. Have you had a close encounter with a UFO?
2. Do you consciously recall (not with hypnosis) the observation of nonhuman entities immediately prior to an abduction while you were outside your home?
3. Have witnesses observed a UFO near your house, vehicle, or tent prior to or during your abduction?
4. Have you experienced at least an hour of missing time following a close encounter with a UFO for which you can find no prosaic explanation?
5. Have you awoken in bed to find beings in your bedroom? Did you move your body or cry out and then become paralyzed?
6. Do you have memories of moving rapidly through the air under someone else's control when you were awake in bed and observed intruders in your bedroom?
7. Do you consciously recall part of an abduction experience?
8. Are you aware of being examined on an alien craft?
9. Have you had recurring dreams or nightmares about alien abduction?
10. Do you occasionally hear strange code-like buzzing sounds in your ears similar to tinnitus, hear telepathic messages, or feel

a strange but familiar sensation that you'll have an abduction experience that night?

11. Have you awoken fearful and unwell, with memories of intruders in your home?

12. Have you awoken with unexplained marks on your body, such as cored-out areas of tissue, triangle-shaped burns, finger-shaped bruises, or a sunburn without exposure to the sun?

13. Have you awoken and found yourself dressed in someone else's clothing or with your own clothing inside out or backward, without a prosaic explanation?

14. If you are female, have you experienced a gynecological problem that you think is related to your abduction/contact experiences?

15. As a child, were you generally happy and without unusual highs and lows?

16. As an adult, are you generally happy and without unusual highs and lows?

17. Can you feel a foreign object in your body that you suspect is an alien implant?

18. Have you awoken with memories of alien abduction and found that you are more sensitive to light?

19. Do you have difficulty falling asleep and remaining asleep due to fear of alien abduction?

20. Have you been diagnosed with chronic fatigue and immune dysfunction syndrome or reactivated mononucleosis?

21. Do you suffer from migraine headaches?

22. Have you awoken with burns, hair loss, or conjunctivitis and memories of an abduction/contact?

23. Has your nose bled immediately following a suspected abduction/contact?

24. Do you crave excessive amounts of salt?

25. Following a suspected abduction/contact, did you ever experience malfunctions of electrical equipment such as lights, digital watches, computers, or appliances, all within a four-hour period?

26. Have you witnessed paranormal activity in your home, such as light orbs, objects flying through the air, pictures flying off walls, lights turning off and on, windows opening and closing, doors opening and closing, and toilets flushing on their own?
27. Are you more or less sensitive, intuitive, or psychic than you were before you had a memory of an alien abduction?
28. Do you possess information about alien technology that you've never read about or learned in your normal environment?
29. Have you had multiple sightings of UFOs up close?
30. Do you have an inordinate fear of alien abduction that affects your everyday life?

Bibliograpy

Part 1

Howe, Irving. *World of Our Fathers: The Journey of the East European Jews to America and the Life They Found and Made.* Harcourt Brace Jovanovich, 1976.

Marciuliano, Francesco. *I Could Chew on This: And Other Poems by Dogs.* San Francisco: Chronicle Books, 2013.

Part 2

Bandler, Richard and Grinder, John. *Frogs Into Princes.*

James, William. *The Varieties of Religious Experience.* New York: The Guildford Press, 1999.

Targ, Russell. *The Reality of ESP: A Physicist's Proof of Psychic Abilities.*

Tart, Charles. *Altered States of Consciousness.*

Part 3

Cialdini, Robert. *Influence: The Psychology of Persuasion.* New York: HarperCollins, 1984.

Hare, Robert. *Without Conscience: The Disturbing World of the Psychopaths Among Us.* Simon and Schuster, 1993.

Lalich, Janja, and Madeleine Tobias. *Take Back Your Life.* Berkeley, CA: Bay Tree Publishing, 2006.

Langone, Michael, editor. *Recovery From Cults: Help For Victims of Psychological And Spiritual Abuse.*

Shapiro, Francine. *Eye Movement Desensitization and Reprocessing Therapy..*

Tobias, Madeleine and Lalich, Janja. *Captive Hearts, Captive Minds.*

West, L. J., and M. D. Langone, M. D. "Cultism: A Conference for Scholars and Policy Makers," *Cultic Studies Journal* 3(1), 1986: 87.

Zimbardo, Phillip. *Influence: The Psychology of Persuasion*. HarperCollins, *1984*.

Part 4

Barks, Coleman. *Rumi: The Glance*. New York: Penguin, 1999.

Zuckoff, Mitchell. *Fall and Rise: The Story of 9/11*. Harper, 2019.

Part 5

Alexander, Eben. *Proof of Heaven: A Neurosurgeon's Journey into the Afterlife*. New York: Simon and Schuster, 2012.

Boone. J. Allen. *Kinship With All Life*. United States: Harper and Row, 1954

Breytenbach, Anna. "Black Leopard and the Animal Communicator, Anna Breytenbach." www.youtube.com.

International Center for Reiki Training. www.reiki.org.

Mancini, Joseph Jr. *Ending the Endless Conflict: Healing Narratives from Past Life Regressions to the Civil War*. United States: Two Suns Press, 2017.

Smith, Penelope. *Animal Talk: Interspecies Telepathic Communication*. Point Reyes Station, CA: Pegasus Publications, 1989.

Smith, Penelope. *When Animals Speak*. New York: Simon and Schuster, 1993.

Targ, Russell. *Limitless Mind*. Novato, CA: New World Library, 2004.

Weiss, Brian. *Many Lives, Many Masters*. New York: Simon and Schuster, 1988.

Part 6

Cynthia Crawford/Dyan, www.etsculptors.com.

DeMarco, Frank. *Muddy Tracks*. Charlottesville, VA: Hampton Roads Publishing Company, 2001.

FREE, The Dr. Edgar Mitchell Foundation for Research into Extraterrestrial and Extraordinary Experiences. *Beyond UFOs: The Science of Consciousness and Contact with Non-Human Intelligence*, vol. 1. Printed by FREE, 2018.

Hansen, Suzy. *The Dual Soul Connection: The Alien Agenda for Human Advancement.* Tauranga, NZ: Skylight Books, 2014.

Howe, Linda Moulton. *Glimpses of Other Realities*, volume 1. Albuquerque, NM: LMH Productions, 1994.

Howe, Linda Moulton. *Glimpses of Other Realities*, volume 2. Jamison, PA: LMH Productions, 1998.

Marciuliano, Francesco. *I Could Chew on This: And Other Poems by Dogs.* San Francisco: Chronicle Books, 2013.

Marden, Kathleen. *Extraterrestrial Contact: What to Do When You Have Been Abducted.* Newburyport, MA: Red Wheel/Weiser, 2019.

MUFON. *MUFON Field Investigator Manual* (Hard copy). Available through the MUFON website. www.mufon.com

Sanchez, Anthony. *UFO Highway.*

Streiber, Whitley. *Communion.* New York: Harper, 2008.

Conclusion

Smith, Pete. "Climate Change Threatens the World's Food Supply, United Nations Warns." New York Times, 8/8/19.

Suggested Reading

Boone, J. Allen. *Kinship With All Life.* United States: Harper and Row, 1954.

Cannon, Delores. *The Three Waves of Volunteers and the New Earth,* Ozark Mountain Publishing, 2011.

Cialdini, Robert. *Influence: The Psychology of Persuasion.* New York: HarperCollins, 1984.

DeMarco, Frank. *The Cosmic Internet.* Charlottesville, VA: United States: Rainbow Ridge, 2012.

FREE, The Dr. Edgar Mitchell Foundation for Research into Extraterrestrial and Extraordinary Experiences. *Beyond UFOs: The Science of Consciousness and Contact with Non-Human Intelligence,* vol. 1. Printed by FREE, 2018.

Marciuliano, Francesco. *I Could Chew on This: And Other Poems by Dogs.* San Francisco: Chronicle Books, 2013.

Marden, Kathleen. *Extraterrestrial Contact: What to Do When You've Been Abducted.* Newburyport, MA: Red Wheel Weiser, 2019.

Murphy, Betsy. *Guide to Caregiving in the Final Months of Life.* Middleburg, VA: TM Brown Publisher, 2019.

Rodwell, Mary. *Awakening: How Extraterrestrial Contact Can Transform Your Life.* United Kingdom: New Mind Publishers, 2010.

Rodwell, Mary. *The New Human: Awakening to Our Cosmic Heritage.* Australia: New Mind Publishers, 2016.

Smith, Penelope. *Animal Talk: Interspecies Telepathic Communication.* Point Reyes Station, CA: Pegasus Publications, 1989.

Targ, Russell. *The Reality of ESP.* Wheaton, IL: Quest Books, 2012.

Tart, Charles. *The Secret Science of the Soul.* Napa California: Fearless Books, *2017.*

Websites and Videos:

Breytenbach, Anna. *"Black Leopard and the Animal Communicator, Anna Breytenbach."* www.youtube.com.

Cory, Caroline. *ET Contact: They Are Here.* Tallahassee, FL: OmNium Media, 2017.

Cynthia Crawford/Dyan, www.etsculptors.com.

EMDR International Association, www.emdria.org.

FREE, The Dr. Edgar Mitchell Foundation for Research Into Extraterrestrial and Extraordinary Encounters, www.consciousnessandcontact.org.

Greyson, Bruce. *"Consciousness Independent of the Brain."* YouTube video, 1:24:18, www.youtube.com

International Center for Reiki Training. www.reiki.org.

International Cultic Studies Association, www.icsahome.com.

Mancini, Joseph Jr., www.explorationsinspirit.com and www.lifetransforminghypnotherapy.com.

Marden, Kathleen. www.kathleen-marden.com

Mutual UFO Network Experiencer Research Team, www.mufon.com.

The Monroe Institute, www.monroeinstitute.org.

Smith, Jacquelin, animal communicator, experiencer, www.jacquelin-smith.com.